How to take the
PANIC
out of public
speaking
2nd edition

Laurie Smale

Incorporating the inspirations gathered from the
thousands Laurie has helped to speak with confidence!

Heartened by the ideas and inspirations in this approach, Niv Neyland penned me this poem. It says it all:

Before I met Laurie, I had plenty of worry
'bout how I would get up and speak
the audience scared me, and even dared me
to be bold and open my beak

Come time to declare, my two cents worth; I share
t'was a frightening experience to tell
Outside I was calm and full of aplomb
But inside reduced to mere jell

Then a meeting with Laurie, and I wasn't sorry
For he unlocked the secrets inside
Of the years of pain, the fear and the shame
And the skeletons I tried hard to hide

Now, I stride onto stage, to the audience, engage
And minus the worry and fear
For the secrets he shared from the vault of his laird
To be sure, are to what I adhere

Laurie, you've got, what others have not
And to this, grateful, I will be:
To find you by chance, thru an internet glance
And remove that knock in my knee

This edition first published in 2020 by
Laurie Smale Presentations
22 Cameron Road
Box Hill North
Victoria 3129
Ph: (03) 9890 3024
Email: laurie@panicfreepublicspeaking.com.au
Web: www.panicfreepublicspeaking.com.au

First published in 1999 by Wrightbooks

A catalogue entry for this book is available from the National Library of Australia.

ISBN: 978-1-922391-18-6

Cartoons by Nick Bland
Project management, cover design and text design by Michael Hanrahan Publishing

Disclaimer
The material in this publication is of the nature of general comment only, and does not represent professional advice. It is not intended to provide specific guidance for particular circumstances and it should not be relied on as the basis for any decision to take action or not take action on any matter which it covers. Readers should obtain professional advice where appropriate, before making any such decision. To the maximum extent permitted by law, the author and publisher disclaim all responsibility and liability to any person, arising directly or indirectly from any person taking or not taking action based on the information in this publication.

Contents

Preface

How to get the most out of this book

Congratulations.

You have just taken the one step that will lead you to boundless speaking pleasure and communicating success – whoever your audience, whatever your topic. The simple ideas within these pages will totally explode the myth that certain individuals among us are born with a monopoly on speaking confidence and you somehow missed out. Follow the tried-and-proven advice this book offers and your speaking success is assured!

This carefully designed approach evolved over many years of helping people overcome their fear of speaking before groups. It is a direct response to questions that crop up again and again, such as:

- "What do I say?"
- "What if I make a fool of myself?"
- "What if I go blank?"
- "What do I do about my nerves?"

These pages tell the stories of people who used to ask these questions, and how they now communicate with confidence. And in their stories, you'll experience *your* story and clearly identify the things that have been holding you back. Gone will be that nagging fear of being found out as a bit of a fake and a fraud. In its place you'll gain a permanent *belief in yourself and your abilities, and you will now have the tools to communicate with confidence.*

Much more than a collection of great ideas, this is a carefully designed and well-tested system that requires you to initially follow each section in sequence to reap the benefits from this mind-opening approach. Therefore, it is essential you first read this book from start to finish to gain an overall understanding of the exciting new path you'll be treading – including the 'Monitoring Your Progress' tasks at the end of each chapter. You can then go back to the beginning and start anew at your own pace, focusing on what is particularly relevant to you.

You'll find each idea builds on the next. Each new understanding will expand your freedom of expression as your long-held anxieties melt away. You'll experience a permanent shift in your thinking as the unbelievable simplicity of it all has you speaking confidently in situations you would never have thought possible.

Tip: Consult the Answer Key on page 196 each time you read one of the Monitoring Your Progress exercises at the end of each chapter. This will not only clarify and reinforce the exciting new ideas you'll be learning; it will give you the confidence to put them into practice!

The difference between this book and a more traditional approach to public speaking is that this book is based on connecting with people on a human level in an *informal,* 'two-way conversational' manner, instead of you struggling against a staid, boring one-way presentation skills correctness! In other words, you'll rediscover the uninhibited expression you had when you were a five-year-old child … before you had this warmth and friendliness conditioned out of you! Most other public speaking courses I've come across tend to focus on the 'do's and don'ts' and technicalities of public speaking with little or no emphasis on being who you are and unlocking the natural talents you already have. With the old way, you're just a talking head and doing it hard out there with little or no engagement with your listeners. So, because the experience is always uncomfortable, your purpose tends to be, "I want to finish as quickly as possible and sit down!" So you stay where you are. The main reason for this is the traditional approach to public speaking tends to focus on addressing the *symptoms* of your fears rather than the *causes*. Harmless as deep-breathing or meditation exercises may be in themselves, they simply don't work when it comes to ridding people of their long-held public speaking fears.

In contrast, each segment of this book is specifically designed to chip away at the real causes of your fears and supplant them with nothing less than a complete paradigm shift that establishes an entirely new foundation of communicating confidence and practical know-how. The central theme of this easy-to-understand approach is to demystify the complexity of it all and show you just how easy a relaxed form of public speaking can be. And guess what? Your listeners will respond in kind! Once you recognise the communicating potential you already possess, you'll be able to rise far above the formalities of public speaking and start connecting with people on a human level.

The conversational tone of this book is quite deliberate, for this approach is about conversing with people in an interesting way, written especially for speakers. And, like a good speech, it embodies the secrets of holding attention using examples of human interest that literally "talk" to you. Thank you to the team at Michael Hanrahan

Publishing, for their unsurpassed publishing expertise in helping me bring this book to life.

Everyone undergoes a sense of initial uneasiness and nervousness when asked to speak before a group – even experienced speakers and coaches like myself! You'll soon learn that feeling slightly apprehensive is normal and vital. But it's the destructive kind of nerves which keep us awake at night that we've got to get rid of. When you feel truly at ease with who you are, have the right mental approach and a simple process to apply, the whole thing becomes an enjoyable experience for both you and your audience. This book reveals all this and will show you how.

Finally, every story and case study in these pages is true. Some names and circumstances have been changed for privacy reasons. My sincere thanks to the countless people who, in discovering themselves and their own freedom of expression because of these practical ideas and inspirations, have helped me discover mine.

Laurie Smale

Monitoring your progress Exercise 1

In order to have you speaking with confidence in any situation, you must first identify the things that have been holding you back. Before you read any further, take time out to list at least 10 public speaking fears you'd like to get rid of.

1. _____
2. _____
3. _____
4. _____
5. _____
6. _____
7. _____
8. _____
9. _____
10. _____

When you revisit this list when you've finished the book, you'll be amazed how these things no longer run your thinking. In their place you'll have a solid belief in your speaking ability and the practical know-how to get your message across in an interesting way with confidence.

CHAPTER 1

A new beginning

You know, it's interesting … most of us have some horrific memory of speaking in public that just won't go away. I don't know if you remember your first attempt at speaking before a group … I certainly do. It was at my friend's 17th birthday party. I recall some kind soul suggesting that 'Laurie give us a speech'. Before I knew it I was standing in front of all my friends, shaking uncontrollably with a microphone in my hand. I can still see the expectant look on their faces. But I let them down badly. My heart was thumping, my knees were knocking, I had a lump in my throat the size of a grapefruit, and the arm that was holding the microphone was waving all over the place. I tried to say something – anything! But nothing came out. Totally humiliated, I sat down without a word.

Six years later I had another go, this time as a featured entertainer at a nightclub in Tasmania. I'd maneuvered my way into the job on the strength of being a finalist in 'Showcase', a well-known national talent quest of the time. I was fine with my set pieces, but the speaking parts in between were my downfall. I could sense the audience wasn't with me. In desperation I waffled on about Tasmania's beautiful lakes and forests, trying to win them back. None of what I was saying had any rhyme or reason. In the end I slunk off stage and headed for the door, but not before the manager stopped me and said: "That was pathetic … Forget trying to be something you're not born to be."

As I trudged home that night I remember thinking, *What he said can't be right … there's got to be an answer!* I stumbled on it twenty years later.

The pain can last years

My Tasmanian experience affected my public speaking confidence for years. Interestingly enough though, I now speak before groups for a living. One of my more impressive stints as a professional speaker was as Master of Ceremonies at the VIP luncheon for the World Masters of Business Congress in the banquet hall of Melbourne's prestigious Melbourne Park in front of 1500 people! This alone puts paid to the notion that some people are born 'natural speakers' and the rest of us are left to wonder at their God-given talent.

It's easy to see a speaker in this sort of situation and find yourself saying 'Wow! What I'd give to have that talent!' But the mere utterance of these words can reinforce the belief that you somehow missed out on this 'gift'. The reality is you're probably looking at the culmination of years of painful trial and error the speaker has endured to reach this point. So, recognise this and don't fall for the age-old trap of comparing yourself to others. They're who they are and you're who you are, so this is the person we have to build on. This learning experience will show you how.

By the end of this book, you will have inherited a total shift in thinking. Yours will no longer be a tortuous journey strewn with fear for I've done all the hard work for you. You'll be walking a new path of confidence you're not even aware of at the moment, and deftly dodge the potholes that will inevitably appear in your way. And as each day goes by, you'll become better and better at getting your message across with confidence.

Stephen Covey had it right when he said, "If you think the problem is out there, stop yourself, because the thought is the problem." Don't let your fears govern your thinking – be the boss of the situation and where you'd like to be.

Four simple steps to put you in control

One major cause of the fear I hear over and over again is the worry-filled period from the moment you hear you've been asked to give a speech – to the moment you have to give it! For many this dreaded lead up is when the panic really sets in. If you can relate to this, the following Four-Step Formula will really help put you in control.

Someone once asked me, "What about you? Don't you lie awake at night worrying about this too? How do you handle it?" And I tell these people that I am just like them. I tell them that when first learning of a speaking engagement, I'm afflicted with the same anxieties and concerns as they are. But these feelings are fleeting, for I now have a simple Four-Step Formula that puts me in complete control of the situation so that I rest peacefully of a night and sleep like a baby. I make it a rule that the very day I learn about a speaking role, before I go to bed that night I have a rough draft of my talk down on paper, as per the following four simple steps. And I can tell you it's a wonderful sense of relief once you've done this, for you're already doing preliminary work on the substance and outcome of your talk. Your mind is now at rest and free to work constructively for you as you go about your day.

So let's look at this simple Four-Step Formula.

Step one: establishing your purpose

During a break in rehearsals of a play I was once in, a young university student said to me, "I can't concentrate tonight ... I'm struggling with an essay I've got to hand in tomorrow and I don't know how to conclude it."

I walked him over to a quiet corner, explaining that I'm in the business of helping people communicate more effectively. I then asked him if the angle he was taking would end up addressing the lecturer's question.

"Yes, I think so," he replied.

"Well, based on what you're trying to say, tell me the message you want to get across ... your argument ... the heart of the matter."

Off the top of his head, Robert gave me a wonderfully concise response.

"There's your conclusion! Weave what you just said into your concluding paragraph – it's the essence of what the essay is all about." Of course, I got him to make sure all his paragraphs supported this central contention too.

Robert was absolutely thrilled that such a simple solution could so decisively solve a difficulty that had dogged him for years. From then on I got him to remember the wise words of our friend Steven Covey: "Always begin with the end in mind."

To be clear and to the point with any communication you must have a straightforward idea of what you want to say, a precise destination where you intend to lead your listeners. And in achieving this, do you want to inform them, persuade them or entertain them, or a combination of these? If you haven't got a crystal-clear idea of where you're heading, you'll sure-as-eggs lose your audience along the way. Cicero, the famous Roman orator, knew the importance of this when he said, "Before beginning, prepare carefully." So first know your purpose ... your destination.

And this 'destination' should embody the very essence and reason for your talk. A young playwright once said to Leonard Bernstein: "I have a fantastic idea for a stage play." Bernstein replied: "I would love to hear it – write it down on the back of your business card and give it to me." Astonished, the young man said, "I can't possibly put the whole idea on the back of a business card." Bernstein replied: "Then you don't have a valuable concept."

Tip: Narrow your focus to give this specific audience what they want. Ask yourself: what motivates these people to be here? What are their needs, their desires and achievements? Keep the responses to these questions foremost in your mind as you formulate your focus sentence.

Spend time reflecting on who your audience members are, their possible frame of mind, and the precise message you want to get across. Now, as I got Robert to do, reduce this message to a single sentence … what I call the 'focus sentence'. This single operation will cut hours off your preparation time, for in one stroke you'll have the essence of your conclusion, the concise message for your listeners. At the end of your talk, all you have to do is echo this sentence. You'll now have a crisp, clear, deliberate ending that adds impact to your presentation and ties it all together. Makes sense, doesn't it?

For example, the overall purpose of this entire book reduced to a single sentence is simply this:

> To permanently replace your fear of speaking before groups with the firm belief that you now know what to say and how to say it with confidence!

Step two: signposting the body of your talk

Now that you know how to establish a concise statement for what you have to say, the second step of our Four-Step Formula focuses on the body of your talk. You need to provide a series of vivid mental signposts to unambiguously lead your listeners along a predetermined path to your 'focus sentence' destination. And what exactly are these signposts? A series of mental joggers like a few key words and phrases, pictures, charts or objects. Placed strategically in view, each of these signposts will suggest what story or case study to share to make a particular point. Each of these mental signposts represents the main idea of a verbal paragraph. You'll glean the ideas you need through study, experience and research, or most of what you want could be in your head. To set up these signposts, simply arrange each central idea so that one example logically follows another and carries your theme forward. Imagine these signposts pointing your listeners in the right direction, so they easily reach the destination you have created for them with your focus sentence.

And how many of these signposts do we need in the average talk? Although there is much truth in the adage 'it takes a lot to teach a little', don't attempt to dump all of your research and knowledge on your listeners in one go. Research shows that audiences can only take in three to five central ideas at any one sitting. After that, their eyes glaze over and they turn off!

Information overload

I occasionally experienced this at university as a mature-age student … many lecturers were distant talking heads, more interested in impressing us with their knowledge than connecting with us on a human level. I remember one singularly uninspiring lecture where the professor assailed us with over 50 overhead images in one session! I recall sitting there totally lost and wondering what it all meant. When he finally finished we couldn't get to the door quickly enough.

In a talk in one of my workshops a lady took us on a lightning tour of 'The Garden'. In five minutes she covered:

- prefabricated garden edging
- how to prune trees
- laying black plastic and woodchips

- installing a sprinkler system

- how to clean yourself and your tools.

Needless to say, we got little from this barrage of information.

The following session we had a rerun. This time we called her talk, 'How to Maintain Your Gardening Tools in Top Condition'. And what a difference! We had a real-life example of what happened when her teenage son used the garden fork and then just threw it in the shed without cleaning it. We had a demonstration, with the actual fork, of how to get rid of caked-on clay and how to lightly oil the fork before putting it away in its rightful place. Even today, when I walk into my garden shed and see bits of dirt on my gardening tools that talk pricks my conscience.

No matter how tempted you are to broaden your listeners' minds with everything you know – don't. Remember your focus sentence, and what you want them to be thinking about or act upon when you step down from the platform. It's best to follow internationally renowned trainer and author Doug Malouf's advice and only expand upon three or four 'must knows' from your array of information. Then, painful though it may be, put the rest aside for another occasion.

Internationally acclaimed author and speaker Bryce Courtenay sums up this second step of our Four-Step Formula succinctly: "An ounce of inspiration is worth a ton of information." And I thoroughly agree with him. Impart some valuable information, sure, but your listeners should be inspired to want to dig further for themselves. They should be queuing up at the end of your presentation eager to talk to you.

Tip: Brainstorm your ideas. Write your focus sentence in the middle of a piece of paper, and then let your ideas flow freely around it. Don't be judgmental at this stage, as this will interfere with the creative process. Even a nonsensical suggestion could generate the exact idea you were looking for!

Step three: use vivid, illustrative examples

You'll notice how I use vivid, illustrative examples throughout this book to make each idea live in your memory and mean something to you. Real-life examples will help you remember what's important. You'll readily relate to each story and visualise each idea in action. In fact, make it a cardinal rule to never proffer an assertion in a talk and then leave it hanging. To be a credible speaker, you must give examples to support what you are saying. You can use your signposts as a starting point for your examples. The late Steve Jobs, founder of the Apple empire and persuasive speaker in his own right, gave very sound advice when he said: "If you want to connect with your listeners make sure all your presentations are evidence based."

Tip: Disparate bullet points are very good for conveying sterile, factual information but no good for conveying complex ideas. There is one thing and one thing only that can do this in a simplified, accessible way and that is a story. Remember our previous example in step two of the lady with the gardening tools talk? How easy was it to understand the complex notions of self-initiative, responsibility and pride in the simplicity of her 'cleaning the gardening fork' talk. No audience will ever complain that you've made things too simple for them!

Step four: motivating people to think and act

And finally, step four of our Four-Step Formula is to motivate people to think and act! Conclude by restating the message embodied in your focus sentence by way of an interesting story, a thought-provoking statement, a helpful summary, or an inspirational saying. Indeed, your conclusions will now be crisp, clear and deliberate.

Make no mistake, for many of your listeners your ending could be a new beginning! For example, with my talk on 'How to

Maximise Your Communicating Potential', I often close with the stirring words of Elizabeth Seton, America's first saint. When I first saw these words I was amazed that someone could encapsulate my whole philosophy in two sentences. Here's what she said: "When so rich a harvest is before us, why do we not gather it? All is in our hands if we will but use it." I then walk off the stage with these words reverberating in my listeners' minds.

> **Tip:** Always signal when you're nearing the end of your talk with something like: "This leads us to a startling conclusion", "Let me close with a story", or, "To sum up let's look at those three steps again". No matter how interesting you are, people love to know the end is near. You'll see them sit up a little straighter with renewed interest in their eyes when they know they're into the last furlong.

This simple Four-Step Formula encapsulates the fundamentals of any successful presentation. It can be tailored to suit the time constraints of the occasion by reducing or expanding the number of central ideas and examples. Note that every chapter in this book embodies these four simple steps and could be delivered as a talk in itself. Reflect on this as you read, so this recurring concept becomes a natural part of your thinking.

Bridging phrases

Throughout the book you'll notice how we move from each key aspect to the next with a little bridging thought or phrase such as: "You're probably wondering how this fits into your situation? Let's explore that for a moment," or, "Now that we've looked at step one let's move on to step two." A lady once said to me that although she'd been lecturing for years and had always carefully planned her presentations, they still seemed a bit jerky and disjointed. For her these little bridging thoughts and phrases were the missing links that had eluded her for years. Think carefully about these linking sentences for they give continuity to what you're saying and carry your talk forward.

Summing up ...

There is no need to learn your entire talk word for word. Your opening, ending and bridging phrases are the only things you need to learn off by heart. Write out a first draft if this helps you, but from then on focus on connecting with your audience rather than memorising your talk parrot-fashion. And the best way to do this is with stories. Focus on your key ideas and how they relate to your audience. Your key ideas could be a series of easy-to-read words, images on a screen, objects or symbols. (You will learn more about openings, endings and using key ideas to rehearse your talks later.)

Although all of this puts you in control and really works, the fact remains that if you're full of self-doubt and lack confidence all of these things are of little practical use. The next chapter will ensure you believe in yourself, recognise your own self-worth and can step forward as someone entitled to be there who knows what they're talking about.

Chapter 1 Key points

Summary of the Four-Step Formula

- Determine your underlying destination. Reduce this to a single focus sentence, the essence of your conclusion.

- Select three to five aspects of your central theme to act as mental signposts that lead to your 'destination.' Keep these ideas focused and avoid information overload.

- Add vivid, illustrative examples and stories to make your message come alive in the memory of your listeners.

- Throw down a challenge! Inspire your listeners to think and act!

Monitoring your progress Exercise 2

True/False

See how quickly you can plan for speaking success by choosing between each public speaking scenario and its correct solution. Before moving on to the next chapter, it is important you check your responses and learn the full facts in the Answer Key on page 196 at the back of the book.

1. The best way to give a convincing talk is to latch on to a central idea and start talking knowing the structure and purpose will evolve all by itself.

2. Your early remarks are nowhere near as important as the impact your final words will have on your audience.

3. Transitional words and phrases are used to transfer your listeners' thinking from one thought to the next as you carry your theme forward.

4. Stick to the nuts and bolts; vivid illustrative examples detract from the real message.

Check your answers and learn!

CHAPTER 2

Getting you right first

Let's just pause for a moment and reflect on you, the person doing the talking. How confident are you within yourself about who you are, where you've been, and where you're at? Over many years of developing the ideas presented in this book I've come to realise that techniques and skills alone are not the answer. When you step onto the platform you've got to genuinely feel that you are entitled to be there. And to do this you must first believe in yourself in order to believe that you can. Shaky self-worth is a central cause of the fear we've got to deal with.

For more than twenty years Carol Tibbet kept her audiences hanging on her every word. Her stories, the drama, the involvement and interaction all combined to entertain and expand her listeners' minds. Carol Tibbet was a primary school teacher.

Yet for those same twenty years Carol lived in abject fear of speaking in public. "It absolutely terrifies me," she confided. "I'm okay in front of my class, but speaking before adults in the staffroom and parent information nights is where I lose it completely."

To cure her of this debilitating condition I had to convince her that the communicating skills she had been using so successfully all those years in front of her class would work perfectly before a group of 'bigger people'. "After all", I told her, "grown-ups are just kids in big bodies. They respond to the same things." The only difference is when her students say something humorous that's a bit borderline she can't encourage them too much – she must play the teacher. But when adults say something that hints of another meaning she can laugh along with them.

"The only thing holding you back from getting what you want is the story you keep telling yourself!"

Anthony Robbins

Here's how Carol gave herself permission to be her mature self when speaking before adults. I asked her to précis a favourite book of hers: *The Velveteen Rabbit*, a moving story of change and renewal as seen through the eyes of a well-loved, then discarded velveteen rabbit. I then asked her to pitch her story to parents who were trying to cope with the pressures of today's ever-changing education system by giving them certain things to look out for in the story – the very techniques she would use with a group of wide-eyed six-year-olds. The result was amazing. I watched that group of adults sit enthralled as they related their situations of change and renewal to the universal principles embodied in the story. When she finished, the applause was genuinely warm and appreciative.

Now when Carol speaks before her peers in staffroom meetings or addresses parents on information nights, her Velveteen Rabbit experience is never far from her mind. She now knows that no-one is there to do her any harm. They are there to hear what she has to say as the person in charge of the classroom. She now simply addresses their concerns using the communicating skills and techniques she's successfully been using with 'younger people' for years. Carol now believes she has something to say and knows how to say it! David W Hutton, author of *The Change Agents' Handbook*, says it all: "Every human being can be persuasive, given something they believe in."

Discovering your passion

Like Carol, I let an inner fear gnaw away at me for decades. For nearly 30 years I was mathematically incompetent. Being dragged to the front of the class each day by old Ludge in year 7 and laid into with the strap for not understanding my algebra homework didn't do a great deal to help. As a consequence, I left school at 13 and went to work in a junk yard. For years I was ashamed of who I was and the poor family I was brought up in. I was ashamed of the pitiful journey I'd travelled. My sense of self-worth was virtually non-existent and I lived in constant fear of being confronted with any form of mathematics. But most of all, I was ashamed of living the lie that I was okay and not being able to tell anyone about it. It wasn't until I had the courage to do something about it 25 years later and go back to school as a mature-age student that I could turn things around and start believing in myself.

Today I stand before audiences and speak with a passion about believing and achieving; I speak with a passion about reaching out for help; I speak with a passion about casting off our fears and tapping into our unlimited potential; I speak with a passion on the wealth of accumulated expertise and life skills within us all. And I speak with a passion about how everyone, with a little help, can communicate with confidence so that people respect and appreciate what they have to say. Do my listeners believe me? You bet they do! They believe me because they're in the presence of an authority on the subject who speaks with conviction. They believe me because they're in the presence of someone who at long last now believes in himself.

> **Tip:** One way to drive home a point is to hammer it again and again with the same phrase in two or three consecutive sentences. It is a well-known fact that repetition helps us retain information

Self disclosure

Notice how I've shared a little of my journey with you here to establish credibility? One of the most powerful ways to create rapport with an audience and win their trust is to let them know you are subject to the same human frailties and vulnerabilities as they are. An example of how you felt scared when you started your first job or came a cropper when you tried to be a 'know it all' will warm them to you as a real person. Simply reinforce any key aspect of your talk with an example from your own experience. Audiences readily relate to the valuable lessons of our trials, tribulations and experiences. Glenna Salsbury, former President of the National Speakers Association in America, says, "If you want to influence people, use the stories that are the turning points for you and bring them to your audience."

Earning the right

And the same thing applies to your particular field of expertise. If you know nothing about scuba diving you don't speak to a diving club about selecting the right equipment, but an expert in communication skills might talk about the necessity of getting your safety message across before you dive into the water. A doctor might talk about what happens to your blood if you ascend to the surface too quickly. And a marine biologist might talk about the fragile nature of the underwater seascape.

Accumulated expertise

And what exactly is this accumulated expertise we mentioned earlier? Put simply, it's anything you've ever experienced. For a period of three years or so I worked on building sites as a bricklayer's labourer and prided myself on the way I kept them supplied with bricks and mortar and anticipated their every need. The bricks were exactly where they wanted them, the mortar was always the right consistency, and the tools were always clean.

Thirty years later I occasionally found myself assisting a cameraman friend of mine when filming on location. And guess what? I found myself drawing on my experience as a bricklayer's labourer all those years ago. I was able to anticipate exactly where Peter wanted his lighting set up or anticipate which camera he needed for a particular sequence.

How many times do we sell ourselves short because we forget that these experiences and skills are transferable – including valuable lessons in what not to do! The fact is you are clever and knowledgeable in many things, and to be an effective communicator it's important you accept this and use this knowledge to your advantage.

Tip: A snippet here and there of something you once experienced, relative to the moment, adds interest to you as a speaker. Not only do your listeners find it interesting, it gives them something to talk about when they later find themselves chatting to you over coffee.

A new image to live up to

Let's further expand this all-important notion of self-worth and believing in yourself so you can step forward with confidence and not feel afraid of being a fake or fraud. A newly-appointed State Manager of a large financial firm once phoned me for some help with presentation skills. The problem, however, had little to do with presentation skills and everything to do with the long-held negative image she had of herself. She even wondered why she had been chosen for the role. Amanda told me straight out, "With no university degree I see myself as a fake." Now if she said this, she believed it. And if she believed it, she would always see herself as a fake. So the first thing we did was get Amanda to recognise her accumulated expertise and see herself in a positive new light. For only when she believed in herself as the genuine article would she be able to speak with conviction, with passion, and live up to the trust others had invested in her by making her State Manager.

During our session I discovered that this notion of a university degree being the 'be all and end all' of success had been drummed into Amanda by her well-meaning parents ever since she was a little girl. But having left school in year 11 to work as a receptionist, she failed to live up to their expectations, and as a result she was not only a great disappointment to them, she was an even greater disappointment to herself. From then on, anything she achieved in life she simply put down to being a fluke. Despite the fact she went on to business school as a mature-age student and topped the class. And despite the fact that she was the main driving force in setting up the multi-million-dollar Queensland arm of this financial firm from scratch.

Amanda was the perfect person for the job. She was an expert in the field, for she had learned everything from the ground up. Little wonder she was chosen to duplicate the same thing in Victoria. And while all this was going on she managed a household and brought up three kids of whom she is very proud. Yet for years Amanda had deemed all of this accumulated expertise insignificant and saw herself as a fake because she didn't have a university degree!

I told Amanda that I'd experienced a similar lack of self-worth for decades, until I had the courage to get my university degree when I was 40 years of age. Proud though I am of this achievement for it helped me think clearly, my greatest lesson was understanding that I could have believed in myself many years before if only I'd known how to recognise my accumulated expertise and not let a 'piece of paper' control my life.

I asked Amanda to imagine herself being introduced as the guest speaker at a large business convention on the topic 'What Financial Services Mean to You'. Then, replaying the essence of what I'd gleaned from our discussion, I read something like the following introduction out loud from an imaginary lectern:

And now it's time to introduce our guest speaker, Amanda Jones, The Victorian State Manager of Trusted Financial Services.

Six years ago Trusted Financial Services was nothing more than an idea whose time had come ... A shoestring business whose main assets were enthusiasm, integrity, and a passion to give the customer the financial service they so desperately need in today's ever-changing world.

With more than 20 years' experience in the industry, Amanda is a proven authority in her field. From channelling enquiries to the right person as a young receptionist with a large bank, to being the main driving force in establishing the Queensland arm of the company, she has learnt all facets of the industry from the ground up. She is an expert in helping small and large organisations throughout Australia better manage their finances.

To share some of her hard-earned insights ...... Please welcome Amanda Jones.

I turned to Amanda and said, "Is this you?"

She smiled wanly: "I guess it is."

I didn't mince my words. "*You guess it is?* Don't you think it's time you recognised your own achievements and self-worth? How many more years do you need to be an authority in your field? Your family, your clients, and your company obviously have faith in you, it's now time you had this same faith in yourself!"

She sat there somewhat stunned for no-one had ever spoken to her like this before. Then the simple logic of it all sank in. Amanda realised she wasn't 'flawed' because of the journey she'd travelled. She could hold her head up high and be proud of all her achievements instead of denying them.

Nowadays Amanda is in control of where she's been, where she is and where she's going. Her obsession with not having a university degree has evaporated. She might tackle it some time in the future on her terms as a part of her self-improvement, but it no longer runs her life. Once we had Amanda believing in herself, her achievements, and her untapped communicating talents there was no stopping her. I phoned her boss about six weeks later to see how things were going as a follow up to our session. "I don't know what you did down there," he enthused, "but the State of Victoria is going great guns!"

Be your own person

Still following this tack, there are other things that, on the face of it, have little to do with public speaking yet deeply affect our sense of self-worth and right to be speaking in front of groups. Worse still, we can feel very vulnerable that the 'truth' could be found out about us while 'on show' up there before the whole group! Let's demolish these crippling notions here and now!

Not long back I helped a young 28-year-old man to overcome his public speaking fears and his story might help you. I'll call him Bill.

As Bill's story unfolded I learnt that as a kid he had been systematically bullied by a bunch of, for want of a better word, thugs. Now even though this ordeal started in primary school, they'd lie in wait for him and one had even held a knife to his throat and threatened him. His mum and dad knew nothing of this and it continued into his secondary years. So he left school to escape this torment. But the higher up he got, he'd always let those with authority above him brow-beat him into things he felt uncomfortable with and didn't know why.

A couple of years ago he found himself in Sydney as a senior executive for a big company. One of his senior colleagues told him he had to give a vital presentation in two days' time to a group of influential people with millions hinging on it. Bill's whole reputation was at stake. "But I don't know anything about this subject," he pleaded. "You'll be alright, just do it," this guy with authority above him said. Bill did as he was told – and experienced one of the most horrific 40 minutes of his life, an experience that continued to scar him until he spent half a day with me.

When I explained to him this was just another type of bullying that had continued all his life and that he was letting himself be pushed around and brow-beaten again – the penny dropped. I told him, "They didn't step forward to do this presentation themselves did they! No! They made you be the bunny and do it! They didn't want their reputation sullied or hurt in any way."

When he understood their selfish motives and bullying tactics he said, "And I thought that my public speaking incompetence was to blame for the disaster, that I was hopeless, that it was all my fault." I explained that anybody – even me – would have failed in that unprepared, pressure situation and that it wasn't his fault. That's why they covered their backs by pushing him into it! I went on to say he could have taken control – he could have said, "As this presentation means so much to the company I need either an extra week to familiarise myself with the situation with adequate research or we get someone else more familiar with the subject and situation to do it."

He admitted that for the past three years he had worn the entire blame for this debacle because these guys had him thinking it was all his fault! Realising that he'd yet again let himself be 'bullied' into something he felt bad about, he decided he would never let this happen again. He would not let the bullies who had run his life in his early years go on controlling his thinking for the rest of his life. And that's just what he's done. Not long back he had to give an informative talk about Melbourne after being posted there from Sydney. He told his senior colleagues that he was going to get someone else to do it as having just arrived he knew little about Melbourne but he'd say a brief 'hello' when his colleague had finished.

For the first time in his life he is in total control of the choices he makes without being railroaded into unfamiliar speaking situations with a sinking heart to talk on things he knows little about. He emailed me saying that he feels liberated because at last he is in control, knows his own worth, and is free from the debilitating shackles of bullying which he'd put to the back of his mind but were central to the cause of his problems.

Another example of letting yourself be pushed around so you question your own abilities occurred with Mary, but this was more subtle. Mary, a school teacher, thought she'd run an idea she had for her 10-minute segment in a forthcoming conference past a colleague who was a bit of a 'bossy boots'. "Oh no, that won't work!" she declared. "I wouldn't do that!"

For Mary there was nowhere to go. That was that. The pronouncement had been made. Mary felt deflated because she had used this idea in her class many times and it worked really well. So she just reverted back to a bland Powerpoint version of her idea.

But to Mary's astonishment, this 'bossy boots' brazenly stole the idea that she'd dismissed so strongly as unworkable and used it in her segment of the conference – to great acclaim! This was a severe blow to Mary's self-esteem, and she carried this hurt with her for quite some time.

Nowadays Mary doesn't fall for the trap of 'running things past people' anymore for their 'approval'. She simply says things like: "No problems, I'll look after that with an example they can relate to," or, "That'll be fine, I'll cover that." If pushed on the content she says things like, "I've got plenty of relevant stuff to choose from," and she leaves it at that.

So, stay in control. Don't let others sow the seeds of self-doubt and ruin your thinking. Be your own person.

It's not all about you

And there are still other causes that can weigh us down and prevent us from being the confident person we have every right to be. I was once talking to a group of importers and exporters when someone called out, "Hey, it's alright for you. You were born with this gift of the gab and confidence – but what about the rest of us?" I thought for a moment then said, "Let me tell you a story."

I then took them on a journey of a little boy who had lost his dad when he was three and wandered through life without a father figure to guide him for many years. It was only when he started his own family three decades later that he was able to discover the joys of being a dad and the things he had missed out on as a child. So confidence did not come easy for young Laurie Smale, and it took many painful years of trial, error and self-doubt before he got himself together. "The person standing before you today," I told this audience, "is someone who knows he is not perfect but has learned to focus on the needs of others instead of constantly worrying about his own perceived shortcomings."

While I was packing my things up, a young man came up to me and thanked me for my talk. I said, "I'm glad you got something out of it."

"No, no," he said, "It means much more to me than that."

Then he went on to tell me an incredible story of what happened to him when he was 17. He arrived home from school one day to find his best friend, his dad, motionless on the floor by the computers. This was the person who had nurtured him and sat him on his knee teaching him everything he knows about computers and life. At first he thought his dad was sleeping, but he soon realised he was gone. Bill went on to tell me that for the past five years he had carried a terrible burden of guilt for the role he had played in the loss of his dad. What had he done wrong? What could he have done to help? Then he looked at me and said, "Your talk today has set me free, for I realise it wasn't my fault and my dad understands this." He thanked me again and disappeared into the crowd.

About three months later I got an email from a Bill from faraway Scotland. I thought, "Who on earth is Bill in Scotland?" Then it dawned on me that it was the young Bill who spoke to me after my talk. He went on to tell me that he was working for a company as a surveyor's assistant in the Scottish Highlands and thought I might like to know this. I was touched. My talk had meant so much to him that he had to let me know he was now walking on his own two feet with his dad by his side.

Sometimes we don't realise just how much of an impression a talk can make on our listeners. And this can only happen when we too are free of the conditioned shackles we've picked up along life's journey.

Tip: Confine painful experiences in your life to the historical pigeonhole where they belong instead of carrying them with you to the grave. For example, Old Ludge, the maths teacher who used to torment me with the strap, has been confined to my 13-year-old pigeonhole, years away from where I am today. Why should I let him go on tormenting me when I'm no longer that little boy? In fact, with the wisdom of hindsight I've turned this dreadful experience into a positive for I now always strive to encourage, uplift, and inspire.

Make no mistake; self-acceptance is a vital key to unlocking your natural communicating abilities. So it doesn't matter what side of the tracks you come from, whether you're rich or poor, or what your level of education; it doesn't matter whether your parents were Spanish subsistence farmers who arrived here with nothing more than the clothes on their backs or you've simply found it tough to get where you are. What really matters is how you see yourself and what value you put on yourself today. Keep in mind that you are this person of value not in spite of, but because of the journey you've travelled. Knowing who you are and where you've been, and all the lessons you've learned along the way will generate a quiet confidence within so you'll walk tall and no longer see yourself as a victim of circumstance. Your listeners will know they're in the presence of someone with self-value who knows what they're talking about. And the exciting thing is your knowledge and expertise are ever expanding.

Most important, you now know your journey is not something to be ashamed of and keep hidden, or something to be fearful of that may be found out. In fact, at the right time and place a bit of self-disclosure of the journey you've travelled will help your listeners relate to you. You'll notice that this is exactly what I've been doing with snippets of my own story in these pages. (For more on this, you can read my book *Finding Me Finding You*.)

To sum up, this book is helping you discover that in many ways your listeners' journeys are very similar to yours. They're sitting there with the same sorts of triumphs, joys and worries running through their heads that you experience. So it's your job as speaker to put all the pressing things of the moment in your life aside and focus on them and theirs. Take them on a brief journey of hope and inspiration. Remember, it's not all about YOU. It's all about THEM.

Don't label yourself a lost cause

One last thing. Beware of well-known psychological/personality tests conducted by large corporations. Although they make lots of interesting and sometimes valuable observations about the different personality types among us, they don't embody the absolute truth about you and your potential for change and growth. I've come across many in my coaching sessions and workshops who have declared that because of their 'diagnosed' personality type they'd be ineffective at public speaking. And many have lived with this inhibiting label around their neck for years. Real damage can be done by these complex diagnostic programs if you are in a susceptible state of mind because of past public speaking failures due to you never having any proper help. When vulnerable, these tests can strike a chord of 'truth' in your mind and reinforce the faulty thinking you've picked up along the way. Administered by highly qualified people the results of these tests come across as factual and totally believable. The scary thing is this ill-founded notion about the limitations of your communicating potential is now set in stone and can be carried with you for ages with no leeway for possible changes in thinking and expansion of your mind.

Let me tell you about Vido and what happened in one of my face-to-face coaching sessions. Now Vido was a senior executive of a large organisation and was terrified of public speaking. "I'm behind the eight-ball before I even start because I'm the personality type who is not much good at communicating in general, especially public speaking," he lamented. This prognosis was backed up by a string of public speaking disasters he'd experienced over the years. So as far as Vido was concerned this was his lot in life and he had to live with it as best he could. I said to him, "I'm a professional who spends his life helping others communicate effectively, and during our chat over the past hour or so I haven't noticed any specific problems with the way you speak. You seem okay to me!"

Somewhat surprised, he said, "That's what my colleagues keep telling me!" I then reminded him that psychological/personality tests are written by fallible human beings and are merely a guide for us to consider. Nothing more than a snapshot in time, they're certainly not something to model the rest of our life on. I reminded him that we are changing all the time as we learn and experience new things. So the last thing we need is our very own personal label that boxes us in and stifles expansion of our minds and capabilities.

This destructive labelling can begin at an early age, even by well-meaning people and those very close to us. As a little boy, my son Richard was a real livewire and into everything. When he was in grade one the coordinating teacher shared her concerns with us of Richard's over-exuberance and inattentiveness. She genuinely believed he had ADHD (Attention Deficit Hyperactive Disorder), which was all the rage at the time. I'm not saying ADHD is not a real condition that affects certain children, for it is; but in those days any kid who didn't fit the behavioural mould of the time was all too quickly diagnosed and put on a 'calming' drug regime to settle them down. Some of these kids stayed on these drugs for years. Worse still, they were labelled as kids with a problem and wore this tag for decades. And this debilitating way of thinking was unwittingly perpetuated by the continuous mention of their ADHD condition by the teachers, their schoolmates, friends and family.

The teacher strongly suggested that professional help was what Richard urgently needed.

As I reflected on the situation, I remembered that as a little boy I too had been full of beans just like Richard and I had turned out okay. As far as we were concerned there was nothing wrong with Richard. He was just a normal little boy who was always on the go and needed to be kept busy. We certainly didn't want to label him for life with a stigmatic ADHD tag! So my wife and I made a pact. We would handle the situation ourselves by looking after him as any caring parents would. We would never mention this in front of his siblings or anyone else. We wanted him to grow up, with our guidance, feeling normal. And guess what? He's grown into a well-balanced, normal man who loves sports and is currently involved in being a sound technician!

When Richard was 19 he somehow got wind of this ADHD dilemma his mum and dad went through all those years ago. One day in the kitchen he said, "Hey dad, I'll be forever grateful for you and mum not labelling me with ADHD when I was little." The sincerity with which he said these few words meant a lot to me.

So make sure you're not wearing some negative label around your neck declaring yourself a lost cause with no hope of public speaking success because of what others or psychological/personality tests may have branded you. Public speaking is not a born gift based on a particular personality type. It's a set of skills we learn like riding a bike, and any 'personality' can do that.

Nourish your self-esteem

Let's lock all this in place with a marvellous little technique I first heard from Australian marketing guru Winston Marsh. When someone asks you what you do with your time, don't sell yourself short. Nourish your sense of self-worth and encourage questions, and comment with an off-beat response that hints at what you do in an interesting way.

During the course of a friendly conversation, I once asked a young woman what she did with her time. She shrugged, "I'm just a systems analyst."

I continued in the same friendly vein, "And what systems do you analyse?"

Her response was telling: "I help manage one of Australia Post's largest databases." Can you see the difference in the two responses? One puts her down while the other lifts her up.

Author Ricardo Semler's wonderful story of the two stonecutters beside the road sums this up beautifully. One was asked, "What are you doing?" Without looking up he grumbled, "I'm cutting stone." The other was asked the same question. He put his tools down, looked the person in the eye and said, "I'm building a cathedral."

So from now on, when you're asked to speak before groups, make sure you step forward as a proud cathedral builder and own the stage. Remember the words of Eleanor Roosevelt: "No-one can make you feel inferior without your consent."

Chapter 2 Key points

- Believe that you are the confident speaker you desire to be – this will become a self fulfilling prophecy.

- Take stock of your 'lessons' and achievements, and acknowledge your right to consider yourself an expert on them.

- Discover your passion and use the stories that are the turning points in your life and bring the principles of these to your listeners.

- Share a little of yourself with your audience.

- When someone asks you what you do with your time, don't sell yourself short. Nourish your sense of self-worth with a positive response.

Monitoring your progress Exercise 3

How much do you value you? Think carefully about your answers to the following questions and decide whether your sense of self-worth is where it should be. There is no answer key to this exercise.

1. Do you tend to put yourself down when someone pays you a compliment?

2. Do you ever feel inadequate when in the presence of other speakers who make it all look so easy?

3. Do you recognise your life experiences as a unique source of wisdom and learnings? Or do you deem the paths you've trodden insignificant and uninteresting?

4. How badly do you want to be able to speak before groups with confidence? What would this mean to you both socially and in terms of your career potential?

5. How much are you prepared to put in to banish your fears forever and communicate with confidence?

CHAPTER 3

The magic of being you

As mentioned earlier, traditional approaches to addressing public speaking anxieties centred more on breathing and relaxation exercises and the like to help you overcome your fears. Unfortunately this only addresses the symptoms and not the ingrained causes of your anxiety so the problem stays as it is. People in my programs tell me that in spite of these exercises, outdated strategies and scare tactics, the fear is still there when they stand up to speak. After many years of helping people communicate with confidence, I've finally isolated one of the overriding causes of the terrible panic that assails them when called on to speak before groups: the fear of getting something wrong. Well, the good news is there's nothing to get wrong!

If you think for a moment, the ideal situation would be to be able to transfer the ease and comfort you feel when talking to family and friends up in front of an audience. In these non-threatening cases the fear of getting things wrong isn't part of your thinking. You just interact and talk in an enjoyable way. But we've been conditioned to leave this relaxed side of us behind when we stand up to speak because public speaking is very 'different' to a friendly, everyday conversation. Instead we become some stilted, stiff and an uncomfortable entity that looks awkward that no-one can relate to. Let's look at ways to undo this untenable situation so that both you and your audience feel relaxed and enjoy each others' company.

Formal versus informal

I once spent half a day with a recently appointed CEO of a large association with a membership of more than 200,000 to turn his long-held public speaking fears around.

Ever since he could remember, Gordon (not his real name) had been extremely fearful of speaking in 'formal' situations. For years he was able to avoid this by handballing each speaking task to someone else simply because he could. But in his new role there was nowhere to hide, for as spokesperson, the collective voice of the group, he was The Man. He was absolutely terrified yet no-one knew it.

The strange thing was he was in complete control and at ease when speaking *informally* on social occasions, like at his daughter's wedding.

He told me, "I had no problems here. I just gathered two or three stories that illustrated the way I felt about my daughter and the company before us and shared them. I enjoyed myself in the telling of these stories and after my speech people told me how good I was. Yet something awful happens in 'formal' business settings for the fear really gets to me and I suffer terribly. I walk to the front hoping I'll survive yet another ordeal."

So why this paradox? Why does Gordon feel at home in an *informal* setting like sharing a few words at a birthday or his daughter's wedding and the exact opposite in the 'formal' ones of the corporate world? What's going on here? Nothing that a slight shift in thinking won't fix. Gordon went on to share an amazing story of a harrowing experience which I later revealed to him held all the secrets to his public speaking success.

It was his first 'formal' presentation in his new role as CEO and there was no room for error. He had to get this right. What's more, it was for an Indonesian Trade Mission and there were all sorts of notable people in attendance. A lot depended on the next 20 minutes, for if he blew this his reputation was shot to pieces. He told me that as he was waiting to be introduced his worst fears were realised. A technician sidled over and informed him that the computer he was about to use had just crashed. "Didn't you have a plan B?" I asked. "Yes I did, but in my nervous state of mind I left the manual overhead version of it back at the office!"

He then heard himself being introduced and broke out in a cold sweat. With a heavy heart he made his way to his dreadful fate on the podium. Then something remarkable happened. As he was about to climb the steps to the sacrificial alter, his eye caught a green environmental shopping back at a colleague's feet. *I wonder?* he thought. A mental flash had him recalling an incident a few days earlier of him giving this colleague a ring binder copy of his overhead images and this man putting them in a green shopping bag to look at later. In desperation he dove into the bag, grabbed the merciful ring binder and said to his startled colleague: "I'll just have a lend of this if you don't mind," and headed for the lectern.

He put his precious ring binder in front of him and opened it, and there, before his eyes were the key ideas he himself had prepared, all in sequential order. With no computer to depend on there was no time for him to step into the role of being 'formal' so all he could do was look at the first image and start talking. In sheer desperation his opening words were, "What a pleasure it is to be here."

He genuinely meant it. Not because it really was, but because he had his life-saving images in front of him! His listeners were unaware of this and responded warmly in return.

Then with nowhere to go but to use the sequential ideas and pictures laid out in the ring binder to jog his memory, he had to paint pictures in his listeners' minds with stories that lived and breathed because the pictures were too small to hold up.

For the first time in his life Gordon spoke in a natural, informal way to this *business* audience without him trying to conform to a 'formal' setting. In fact, without realising it he was the friendly, accessible person who spoke so warmly at his daughter's wedding. And his audience couldn't help but respond in kind.

When he arrived at the last image, logic told him to tie it all together by saying, "What this all means is … ", and his pre-planned conclusion came out of him just waiting to be said. Relieved beyond measure for having survived the ordeal, Gordon made his way to the safety of his table with warm applause ringing in his ears.

The funny thing was, Gordon put the remarkable success of this presentation down to everything but himself. It was the audience, or the ring binder, or even the venue – everything but him! I explained that through this nightmare experience he had stumbled on one of the most important secrets of all: every talk you ever give should be prepared, rehearsed and delivered in an *informal*, friendly, approachable way. Who likes to be in the presence of some 'formal', stilted entity trying to be something they're not? We all enjoy being in the presence of a speaker we can relate to and who is real.

Gordon now realises that what happened on this occasion was precisely what he had done at his daughter's wedding. He had gathered three stories to share, one when she was little, one about her life now and her relationship with her new husband, and a speculative one on how things should be. Here each of these stories suggested the next, without having to memorise everything word for word, precisely what happened on the 'ring binder night' where each image brought to mind what story and case study to share and what point to make. In retrospect, he clearly sees what he did. Gordon has now wiped the term 'formal' from his thinking with regards to speaking before business groups – it had been a terrible millstone around his neck for as long as he could remember. He now prepares and delivers all his presentations in the same *informal* way he did with his daughter's wedding and the 'ring binder' awakening. Make sure you do the same.

Not long after this I received the following email from Gordon:

Good Morning Laurie,

I'm very pleased to report that my speech at last night's networking event for our association far exceeded my expectations. I went very well and I experienced that same 'good feeling' afterwards that I had only experienced once before 'by accident' – at the 'ring binder' occasion.

The difference is, this time I did it by design.

We had 150 people along last night so it was an important occasion for me to represent our association well.

Thanks again for your valuable assistance in helping me to overcome my long-held problem of believing in myself.

Kind regards,

Gordon

Make friends with your audience

So let's build on this. Former Australian Businesswoman of the Year, Sara Henderson, admitted she used to be absolutely petrified at the thought of speaking in public. Her first attempt at public speaking was a total disaster. She simply walked round the back of the country hall and threw up. But the audience were not going anywhere. Sara had nowhere to go but walk back and face them. So all she could do was tell her story of the untimely death of her husband and how she found herself managing a large Queensland cattle station with three little kids to bring up.

She ended up becoming a speaker of note and sharing her story of success with thousands. One telling remark that sits well with my philosophy is something I heard her say in an interview when asked about her initial fear of public speaking: "The trick I've discovered," she said, "is to chat with your listeners as if they're your friends." There it is again! … the magic of being *informal*.

I discovered this magic little 'trick' myself. For many years, like Gordon, I was locked into a formal approach to public speaking because like many others I'd been conditioned to think that giving a speech was all about being 'formal' and somewhat distant and 'serious'. As a consequence I struggled trying to be something I'm not. I tended to be more concerned about what I looked and sounded like than actually connecting with people as the real person I am on a human level. As former Channel 7 newsreader Malcolm Gray so aptly puts it: I was more self-centred than audience-centred. That is, I was more focused on my perceived shortcomings and getting everything right than what my message meant to my listeners. I guess it was a throwback to the days of the silver-tongued orator when people would sit for hours and be impressed by such things as pace, pitch, modulation and grand gesturing. Today the buzzword is 'body language'. I've come to realise that nowadays people simply want a warm human being to talk with them.

One particular night as I was sharing the one and only image I have of my father, stored in the mind of a little three-year-old boy, I connected with my listeners in a way I'd never experienced before. It was a wonderful feeling to have all those people sharing my emotions in a tangible way. Even more remarkable, my public speaking panic had somehow left me.

That night I couldn't sleep. I remember lying awake reflecting on exactly what it was that I had done different – then it dawned on me. I had shared this story with those people as if I'd been talking to them over the dinner table. Like Sara Henderson, I'd had a friendly conversation with them. There was no 'put on' public speaking voice here, no concern about what my arms or hands were doing. I was just talking as one with them, sharing something I cared deeply about. I remember thinking out loud, "I wonder if I can teach this to others?" As luck had it, two nights later another public speaking opportunity presented itself where I could affirm that the first time was no fluke. I shared the following story with this new audience to make the point that sometimes we have to take things into our own hands. I shared this story with this different audience to prove to myself that this was an approach worth pursuing. Here's how the story went:

> As a part of my chequered career, I once did a four-year stint as a postman at the South Yarra Post Office in Melbourne … the days when hand-written letters were the way people communicated. Like most things I've ever tackled, I took immense pride in my work.
>
> One day, a Christmas card from Canada addressed to a customer in my area was returned to my desk with the word 'deceased' scrawled across the front of the envelope in red ink. Now the strict rules of the postal system required me to add "Return to Sender" to the insensitive front message and send it back to Canada. I remember sitting there stunned, thinking: *There has to be a more sensitive way of handling this sad news. After all, I knew this friendly man who had died. We used to enjoy a regular chat.*
>
> So I took it upon myself to cover the insensitive announce-ment with a white sticker, and after some discreet enquiries, put the letter in a new envelope with a note of my own: "Sadly Mr Jones is no longer with us. He died peacefully in his sleep three weeks ago. Laurie, Postman, Round 7, South Yarra Post Office." I popped this in the mail and thought no more about it.

A couple of months later I received a letter from Canada addressed to Laurie, Postman, Round 7, South Yarra Post Office. I wondered: *who on earth would know me in Canada?* When I opened it, I found it was a letter of profound gratitude, thanking me for letting them know their dear friend was now at rest as they had worried about him for some time. They were particularly thankful for the thoughtful way I had conveyed the sad news.

I was touched. All the money in the world could not buy the way I felt at that moment.

And my listeners were touched too! The first time was no fluke – it worked! Now, as a direct result of this simple discovery, thousands of people communicate with confidence in a way that they never dreamed possible.

One night I was sharing these ideas with a group of business people when a lecturer from one of Melbourne's leading business colleges said: "What you say is absolutely true. I've been standing behind that lectern for six years now and no matter how hard I try, I just never seem to connect with my audience on a human level. The amazing thing is, in an informal tutorial setting we laugh and interact in a way that just doesn't happen in my lectures."

I then asked him if he'd ever thought of approaching his lectures in the same *informal* manner. He admitted that he'd never given it a second's thought. Like most of us, he'd always seen the two situations as totally different entities. He now knows otherwise. His lectures now reach people because of his new understanding and approach.

TIP: If you find yourself speaking behind a lectern, don't use it as a shield to hide behind. Accept that it's there because it has to be. If possible, stand beside it so people can see you.

Let me tell you what happened to a friend of mine, Sean, who is a teacher, a poet, and an experienced public speaker. One night as he got up to speak I invited him to try something new, to think of his talk as a 'friendly conversation' rather than a formal speech. Steeped in the old school of thinking, this concept was entirely new to Sean and momentarily threw him. He then said an interesting thing, "Well, since I'm in conversation mode I may as well relax."

What happened next was amazing. His whole body seemed to loosen up. He took on a relaxed air and he smiled. Instantly gone was that subtle public speaking 'correctness' that tends to set up a barrier between speaker and listener. Sean went on to share his ideas on 'The Power and The Passion of Poetry' as if talking to friends over coffee. This approach had us feeling relaxed, involved, and receptive to what he was saying. That night Sean threw off shackles he wasn't even aware he'd been wearing. He now talks to groups of people with the natural freedom of everyday conversation. This is something that's certainly well within your grasp too.

A friendly conversation

So here's what to do to discover this freedom for yourself. From this moment on, never again should you think in terms of giving a speech, or, heaven forbid, delivering a lecture! Change the terminology and you'll permanently change the feelings. From now on your mental approach should be: "I'm going to relax and enjoy a friendly conversation with these people." This one simple step will have a calming effect on your listeners and have them saying to themselves: "I feel comfortable with this person because they're talking to me personally."

You've probably been a part of an audience and experienced these feelings before. You've found yourself nodding in agreement at some thought, suggestion, or question put to the audience and felt a real part of the presentation. And you've probably put this down to the speaker being a 'natural'. Well, that is indeed true. But so are you in your own way. All you have to do is converse with your listeners in the same friendly way you do with family and friends.

This one simple conversational step decisively deals with another major cause of ingrained public speaking panic because it neatly side steps all of the outdated 'rules'!

Kiss the panic goodbye!

As with the example of Gordon earlier in this chapter, one of the greatest fears people have when speaking before groups is making an absolute fool of themselves because they're terrified of not being 'formal' enough and getting some of the all-important 'formalities' wrong. But getting *what* wrong? I'll say it again: I firmly believe all those nebulous public speaking rules and regulations that have been handed down to us from bygone eras are outmoded to the point we don't even know what they are! Yet because all these 'do's and don'ts' remain in print we've been conditioned to accept them as the gospel on public speaking and this is how it always has been done and always will be done. People even lie awake at night worrying about them!

What are your listeners really thinking?

In my seminars I get my listeners to help me list on the board all the things that are bothering them with regards to public speaking, one of which is the feeling that most audience members are there to judge them and do them harm. Referring to this list, I then say: "These are the things on your mind when you get up to speak. What are the things on your listeners' minds when they are sitting there to listen?"

This always throws them somewhat, so I ask again: "What things are running through your *listeners' minds* as they sit there waiting for you to speak?"

Now we start getting tentative comments like, "Overcome their fear of public speaking," "Gaining confidence," and so on. With a little goading, we learn of other things that could be on their minds, such as, "That looming mortgage payment," "A sickness in the family," "Job security," "Relationship problems," "The soulmate of their dreams," and so forth. They soon discover that the last thing on their listeners' minds is the speaker's list of personal public speaking concerns. What the listeners really want is a bit of hope! They want answers and practical inspirations to give them security and be successful in some way. Once you are aware of this – and free of your own fears – your talk can introduce them to all manner of exciting possibilities. And you can only reach out and do this when you understand that it's not about you at all, it's all about *them*.

> **Tip:** So even if you have all the answers, keep the heat on your listeners for their input. Every so often throw them a question. This takes the pressure off you and gets them involved. Don't be in a hurry for answers. Give them time to think. It won't be long before someone says something to either confirm or expand on the idea under discussion.

Sadly, this overwhelming burden of trying to get it all 'right' stifles who we are as natural human beings and goes on feeding the fear. When we get up to speak we are consumed with what other people might be thinking about us instead of what we are going to say in relation to them and their problems. The panic takes over because our focus is solely on external technical and mechanical things, such as pace, pitch, modulation, gesture, posture, the correct use of notes, and on and on it goes.

What's more, we are conditioned to think our audience is a bunch of merciless critics ticking all these things off on some mental evaluation sheet. What hope do you have of connecting with people on a human level if this is your state of mind whenever you stand up to speak? We've got to change this state of mind into something much more friendly and engaging.

Out with the old and in with the new

So let's pause for a moment and recap on just how important all of this is. Take the whole lot of these inhibiting rules and regulations that are hard to pin down – including the term 'giving a speech' – and throw them out the window. In doing this, you will be throwing a major cause of the panic out too! Remember, the mere thought of giving a speech can evoke a whole raft of negative feelings about getting things wrong. I repeat, by changing the terminology, you are changing your feelings as well. By thinking 'friendly conversation' rather than 'addressing a group', you've rewritten the rulebook and cast off the shackles of the past. The only public speaking rules you're going to worry about from this point on in your life are common sense and good manners. It really is that simple.

Notwithstanding all of this, people still say, "This all sounds great, but what about my nerves?"

And to that I say, "Well, what about your nerves?" We are beings with a nervous system. In any area of life where there's a bit of a challenge we can't perform at our best unless stimulated by normal, healthy excitement and the occasional rush of adrenaline. Think for a moment of the athletes who train for many years for their moment of glory at the Olympic Games. Imagine the mix of adrenaline and excitement as they nervously wait in the starting blocks. These people tell us all the time that they can't perform without it. Speaking before groups is no different. Once you've got yourself right and know what to say and how to say it in an interesting way, you'll be on firm ground and quickly learn to enjoy the experience.

But I've developed some secret strategies to transfer your initial nervous energy to your listeners within the first minute of your talk so they sit up and listen. A bit like taking part in some sporting event where once the whistle blows you're in the game and okay.

It's what I call breaking through the adrenalin barrier so you deal with being pumped up and on edge with the first words you say. Then start enjoying yourself! But one thing at a time … These sure-fire strategies will all be explained in the next chapter.

So to sum up: by throwing all those formal 'do's and don'ts' out the proverbial window, you've thrown a major cause of your panic out with them – for good! You're now your own person and no longer have to give in to a set of rigid rules or the well-meaning opinions of others. Your fear of getting things wrong or making a fool of yourself no longer runs your life. You're free to be your interesting, fallible self and relish the normal, healthy excitement and rush of adrenaline we all face with any challenge.

Body language: 'doing what comes naturally'

"But," you may still be wondering, "aren't all those intricate facets of public speaking and body language important? Don't we need a guide, some sort of benchmark against which to measure ourselves in communicating effectively?"

Yes we do … but the wonderful news is it all comes naturally.

Let me tell you about Bruce Duncan. Bruce was invited to stand up in one of my workshops and tell us who he was and what he hoped to get out of the session … a harmless enough request. Totally locked into the mindset of public speaking being synonymous with abject terror, Bruce came across as a quivering wreck. He told me afterwards: "I just wanted to get it over and done with and sit down." Yet not 10 minutes later I witnessed a miraculous transformation in Bruce's communicating abilities.

We had just stopped for a coffee break when I noticed Bruce engaged in a lively conversation with a group of his fellow partici-pants. I tuned in to what he was saying.

He was reliving what had happened at the cricket the Saturday before. " … Anyway, Ponting hit the ball," he enthused … "And as I followed its path, I could see that it was heading for the grandstand

... straight for me!" His listeners could 'see' the ball as it soared sky-wards. "Now I don't know why, but I leapt to my feet and caught it! And sixty thousand people went berserk!" At this stage Bruce was on his feet with an imaginary cricket ball in his hands above his head.

"What did you do?" someone asked.

"I'll tell you what I did ... I sheepishly threw the ball over the fence and sat down ... Talk about feeling embarrassed!" As he spoke Bruce intuitively enacted the whole thing as if he were there again. He leapt to his feet to catch the ball, he projected the roar of the crowd and he conveyed his acute embarrassment as he sat down again. There was nothing stilted and mechanical here. His body language, his pace, his pitch and modulation just 'happened' and complemented what he was saying perfectly. It was hard to believe that this was the same self-conscious person who had struggled to tell us who he was a few minutes earlier.

After the break I said to him, "During the break I couldn't help but tune into your cricket story... Why didn't we have that Bruce Duncan up here before?" And he said something quite profound, yet a familiar refrain: "I didn't know we could speak like that in front of people. I thought public speaking was something else, something more formal."

I then explained that we'd just experienced the real Bruce, not someone trying to emulate a public speaker – whatever that is. In fact, I encouraged Bruce to keep his 'cricket story' as a permanent reminder of just what it means to be himself and connect with people on a personal level.

As he sat there I could almost hear the penny drop as the meaning of all this hit him. Then and there he replaced the misguided notion of trying to be a public speaking clone with a new understanding of himself and the natural way he speaks. Since then I've experienced Bruce speaking to large audiences on a number of occasions. His examples may be different, but essentially he is the same guy who so effectively relived the story of the cricket during a coffee break. There's no doubt in Bruce's mind that this newfound freedom of expression enables him to command interest and engender respect – a far cry from the frightened individual who stood up to introduce himself in my workshop.

Body language and all those nuances of public speaking will come to you spontaneously and intuitively if you let them. And the easiest way to do this is to relive your examples from memory.

> **Tip:** Respect other people's constructive criticism with grace, but only take on board those ideas you feel comfortable with and that complement your personality and style.

But I can't tell stories!

Notwithstanding the above example, you'd be surprised how many people persist in telling me, "But I can't tell stories!" And I say, "When you arrive home from work or a day's activities and someone asks, 'How was your day?', how do you respond? I'll bet you find yourself answering with something like: "We had a bit of drama after lunch … " I went on to say they'd probably find themselves reliving this 'happening' in a spontaneous way by painting mental pictures, sharing feelings and paraphrasing what was thought and said.

"Oh, yes I do that," they say.

"Well – you can tell stories!"

So it's important to keep in mind that telling a story and reliving a happening to family and friends is one and the same thing. And you've been doing this effectively all your life, just like our friend Bruce had been doing only he didn't know it!

To make it easy for you, think of the stories you'll use in your talks as nothing more than you reliving a relevant 'happening' to humanise things and help your audience relate to what you are saying.

Two-way communication

Often people ask, "But how can you have a two-way conversation with an audience when you're the one up there doing all the talking? I thought a conversation was an interactive thing between two people where you say something and I react to it." My response to this is simple. If you believe you're having a two-way conversation with your audience, they'll believe it too. You'll see your listeners nodding their heads as they find themselves responding to 'feeler' questions like, "Anyone live in Tasmania?", or, "Who can relate to that?", or, "Any idea why this is important?" Feeler questions help create a two-way rapport and allow people to warm to your natural style because they are involved. Most importantly, both you and your listeners will feel comfortable interacting with one another in such a non-threatening environment.

Make no mistake: we tend to trust and feel at ease with people we sense are just like us, and a friendly conversation with your listeners that radiates sincerity is the best way I know to achieve this feeling. Our friend Stephen Covey encapsulates this beautifully: "The more authentic we are the more genuine is our expression."

Ask lots of questions

The problem with many speakers is they are often more interested in impressing their listeners with their infinite knowledge and how clever they are than imparting something of real value the audience can relate to. Don't be a talking head. Get them to come up with the answers themselves.

A head nurse of a major training hospital once told me how tough she found keeping young nurses interested in the courses she was running. "It's a never-ending battle, and I'm glad when each session is over," she told me.

When I enquired further I found Jennifer had been the one doing all the talking and imparting all the knowledge with little or no buy-in from her trainees. She'd lay out all the instruments, 'plastic patients' and electronic devices, then walk her trainees through everything, explaining as she went. The pracs were just a little better as they incorporated hands-on involvement.

"I'm at my wits end," she confided. A big problem was she firmly believed she was born with some fatal public speaking flaw of not being able to connect with an audience which couldn't be rectified. I turned this faulty thinking around with a simple suggestion. I said, "Instead of you coming up with all the answers, put some friendly pressure on them by asking questions such as: 'Has anyone got any idea what this instrument might be used for?' Or, 'What does this represent?'" By asking questions, their minds become involved in the learning. The fact is, when we come up with the answers ourselves we own them and they mean something to us. We become *active* participants instead of half-hearted *passive* learners just filling in time.

Immediately Jennifer could see what she had been doing wrong all these years by not encouraging them to ask questions, think, suggest and explore. Even though Jennifer knows all the answers, she now guides her charges to seek these answers out themselves. All the pressure is now on them and it becomes an enjoyable learning experience all round.

Tip: Always strive to encourage, uplift and inspire. When someone has the courage to answer a question from the audience, ensure your response is always positive: "Great answer, but not quite what we're after"; "Any other suggestions ... ?"; "Spot on!" By keeping your acknowledgments positive, people will feel safe and will be eager to contribute. No-one is going to put their hand up if every time someone does the person is made to feel bad.

Different speaking hats

You still may be grappling with the idea of bringing the casual way you interact with people every day up in front of a group of business people at an important function. "They're two different things," you persist. Well, they are, but they're still creatures of emotion. During the course of a day we wear a number of different communicating hats, yet things seem to sort themselves out naturally. It just happens.

For example, you may be walking down the street having a laugh with a friend about something that happened at work when you bump into a couple of old folk you know who have just lost a loved one. Your whole approach instantly changes. Gone is the carefree spill of ideas of a moment earlier. Your ideas and words are measured as you intuitively react to the situation. You even become a sharer of silence. Then at lunchtime an enthusiastic teenager at McDonald's has you responding in a very different manner as you place your order, and later that day you find yourself passionately expressing an idea at a lively committee meeting.

In all these cases you are instinctively responding to the chemistry of the moment. You didn't have to 'put on' anything.

There is, of course, a certain amount of common sense to all this. As I mentioned earlier, at one stage I spent a period of time working as a bricklayer's labourer. Even today I feel at home with the colourful lingo used on building sites should I find myself in that environment, but my common sense prevents me from speaking like that in the wrong situation. And the same thing applies to our approach when speaking before groups.

Be aware of these intuitive speaking hats you wear during the day, and be aware of the one you'll wear for your next talk. This will define your all-important *approach* to the situation although you'll still be talking as the real human being you are.

Tip: As a general rule, I try to dress a notch or two 'above' my audience. I find this adds to the expectation that they're in for something special. Avoid flashy jewellery or distracting adornments as they tend to focus attention away from you and your message.

Would the real you please stand up

I had just finished dinner and was about to step forward as keynote speaker at a large conference when a dining companion leaned across the table and said, "Who will you be when you're up there? The same person who is talking to me here or someone else?"

Intrigued, I enquired why he asked this.

He told me he had once seen the iconic actor Laurence Olivier interviewed on television and it was Henry IV speaking. And he saw a similar thing with a Peter Sellers interview. Sellers wore a German helmet and spoke with a funny German accent for the entire discussion.

Now this is interesting. Revered doyen of professional speaking in Australia Joan Saxton once told me that for some reason few actors make good public speakers. "They're very good at using other people's words and being other people's characters," she said, "but not very good at using their own words and being themselves."

Luckily at that stage I'd discovered how to be the imperfect but unique person I am.

"What you've experienced around this table," I told my dining companion, "is what you're about to experience up there."

Finding your own style

Extending this further, like the rest of us you have probably been told to "Find your own style" or "Be yourself" – but no-one shows you exactly where to find it or how to be it. During a coaching session I once asked Russell Harrison, one of Australia's most successful insurance brokers and member of the legendary Million Dollar Round Table, what he thought the secrets of creating rapport with an audience were. He thought for a while, and then said, "The speaker has the audience's interest at heart and I guess he is being himself."

"True," I said. "And how do you do that?"

He laughed. "That's what I'd like to know! There are so many things to worry about up there that being yourself gets lost in the fear." I then shared some of my simple insights with Russell. Now when Russell speaks, people sit up and listen because he knows the elusive secret of how to be himself. Allow me to let you in on this illusive secret too!

As illustrated previously with Bruce's spontaneous 'cricket story', when you speak to close friends and family you are at your most expressive because you don't feel threatened. You instinctively have people visualising things, feeling things, and are paraphrasing what was thought and said. That's how animated conversation works. I see it all the time with people sitting at curbside cafes and the like. They laugh, they're animated, they interact, and they're alive! Yet often, when we witness these very same people speaking before groups they seem to leave all this naturalness behind and come across stilted and stiff. If I were to say to you, "Is there another way you can speak and be the warm human being you are other than by speaking as you do in these non-threatening situations?" you'd honestly have to say, "No, there's not." Oh, you can take the panic-strewn path of trying to be a technically perfect public speaker if you wish, but I can assure you your listeners want to feel as comfortable with you as they do when you're speaking to them around a coffee table. That's how to weave your unique brand of communicating magic and win their respect. So it's just not true that you can't be a warm and friendly speaker – it's a matter of helping you understand in a permanent way that these two situations are the same.

Influencing people on their wavelength

Let's look at that coffee table scenario again and cement this understanding permanently in place so that you have your audiences seeing, feeling and hearing exactly what you are saying as they would in those friendly situations. Research shows that in everyday conversation it is the three characteristics of seeing (visual), feeling (kinaesthetic) and hearing (auditory) that trigger all our other senses. It doesn't concern us here which of these characteristics is more dominant in you; all we need know is that everyone uses all three of these seeing, feeling and hearing traits to a greater or lesser extent. And this is the crucial link in understanding why you effortlessly connect with friends around that coffee table and why you'll soon be doing the same with your audiences! By weaving each of these three characteristics into your examples you'll ensure your audience sits up and listens because they'll be reacting and responding to what comes naturally. And doing this is easy. Just be conscious to include them as you tell your story. Remember that these three traits are your listeners' hot buttons and they're just waiting for them to be pressed! Without this happening they remain disconnected from you and what you are saying.

Let's try it with you. Think for a moment of a recent happening you experienced. As you think back on it you clearly see the images of that event ... You experience the feelings of the time as if you were there ... And you hear the things people were saying and the thoughts that were running through your head. For example, I once took my six-year-old boy Richard to a day of activities at our local swimming pool. He'd been excited about this for days, but when we arrived and he saw all the people he had a panic attack. He was too scared to go in, and there was nothing I could do to change his mind. When I think about it now, I can see him crouched behind a bush in the garden and me carrying him in to explain the situation to the lifeguard. I can feel my frustration as I thought, *I'm going to have to take him all the way home again.* And I heard the reassuring words of the lifeguard as she knelt down and said, "Richard, we've got some wonderful videos to show you and a big friendly pool monster you can ride on."

This did the trick. "See you dad," he said, and he was off!

Now, could you see that frightened little boy hiding in the bushes and his frustrated dad carrying him inside? Could you empathise with the feelings of the situation, with me thinking, *This is all I need … now I'm going to have to take him home!* And could you hear the lifeguard saying "We've got some great videos to show you and a big friendly monster you can jump on in the pool." In short, you related to the story because these three things triggered your natural interest and helped you relate by stimulating flashbacks of similar circumstances in your own mind. This naturalness is the very essence of communication, the key to influencing people on their wavelength. Yet in front of people this naturalness has been formalised and conditioned out of us. I've actually witnessed speech critics telling speakers not to be too conversational! And you've experienced the results – speakers standing there like reporters delivering their facts and sterile information, oblivious to the natural stimuli that help us connect on a human level. A speech should be a two-way dialogue, not a one-way monologue. If only they knew – these people have their own version of the magic but no-one has shown them where to find it.

From now on you'll tune in to the ways people express themselves in everyday situations. What you've been doing naturally for years will now be clear to you. You'll visualise the pictures. You'll experience the feelings. You'll be aware of how we paraphrase our thoughts and act out a situation when we describe it. Remember that these three characteristics are the hot buttons that hold our interest and appeal to our hearts and minds. Remember also that these traits register differently with each person in your audience, so don't run the risk of leaving anyone feeling indifferent. Simply duplicate the naturalness of everyday conversation and you'll breathe life into your examples and in some way push everyone's button. And isn't this what I've been doing with the examples I use throughout this book? Every one of them is a real-life example where you see events, you experience feelings and you hear what was being said.

Tip: In a business presentation you could activate the auditory 'sensory button' by giving whole departments a 'speaking voice'. For example, with a talk on effective inter-department communications you could refer to a flow chart and say: Administration says, "Hold on a minute, we're not moving until the correct forms are filled out." And over here the Sales Department says, "But we can't ask our customers to hold off buying from the competition while Administration sorts out their paperwork!" ... Yet another way to humanise your talk and help people relate to what you're saying.

Suitable for any audience

Right now you might be thinking, "Gee, a friendly conversation ... Hey, my audiences are serious people ... This conversational approach would never fit into the culture of my organisation ... I'd be too vulnerable." But to that I say, "Who said information had to be delivered in a formal, stilted, boring way?" If we want to hold interest and influence people, we've got to bring what we say to life. We have to generate trust and respect so that people appreciate what we are saying.

During a personal coaching session, the Mayor of a large municipality wondered how this conversational approach would sit with the seriousness of a Citizenship Ceremony and the dignity of his office. "I've always found these ceremonies rather staid and formal affairs with me just going through the motions," he admitted. "If something could be done about this I'd be more than grateful."

I then got him to revisit the last Citizenship Ceremony he had presided over and imagine himself opening proceedings with something like the following words:

> I recall standing at my first Citizenship Ceremony early this year with the objective of fulfilling my Mayoral duties and getting the formalities over and done with. But then something happened. As I presented my first certificate of Australian Citizenship to a young Cambodian, his tear-filled eyes caught mine. In an instant I understood the pain and torment he'd left behind in his war-torn country. In an instant I understood his eternal gratefulness to be accepted as an integral part of our free and democratic society. When he returned to his table he reverently placed his certificate against a vase of flowers so that he could look at it with pride. Our National Anthem gained a deeper meaning for me that day. Ladies and gentlemen, it is indeed a deep honour to bestow Australian Citizenship on the following recipients …

"Boy!" the Mayor said. "Pity we can't bottle that!" And I said, "There's no need to. All you have to do is replay from memory in a free-minded way, a similar experience of your own." Since then he hasn't looked back.

A school principal of a well-known secondary school once told me that when she has to give a 'formal' address to the power brokers in the Education Department she injects an *informal* element to it by humanising her dry information with one or two pertinent case studies relived from memory and uses these as a central theme to refer to as an example. She said this approach works wonderfully for her.

Humanising technical information

Accountants and technical people often have difficulty with this conversational approach to speaking. "This is all too airy-fairy for us," they tell me. "We're only interested in the facts and figures; the nuts and bolts." But neither of these groups lives by logic alone. They, too, are creatures of emotion. I remember helping an automotive engineer who was particularly concerned about a presentation he had to give on an exciting new braking system his team had developed. He intended to simply stand up and tell his audience about the mechanics of the thing and how it worked. I asked him, "Are you excited about the project?"

"Oh yes!" he enthused.

Building on his enthusiasm, we managed to breathe life and passion into his 'engineering' presentation. We breathed life into it by putting together a profile on each team member's personality and outlined the qualities that brought them together. Then I got him to relive from memory in a logical sequence some of the trials, surprises and inspirations that had occurred to these real people as the project had progressed. By the time he had finished, his listeners not only had a clear idea of how the device worked and where it was going, the story meant something to them on a human level. He told me that other engineers later came up to him and expressed how much they had enjoyed his talk!

Another gentleman in one of my workshops gave a talk on how vital it is to do your all-important safety-check before enjoying water skiing. He told the audience about his long-haired surfie mate Steve, who would pull up at their Lake Eildon camp site in his gaudy panel van and unwind himself from the front seat. "Where's the ski stuff?" he'd ask and saunter over to the boat.

We then heard how his scruffy-looking friend would always meticulously check every piece of equipment – including the towrope for signs of fraying – before they went for a spin.

Kelvin concluded his talk by reliving an incident he'd witnessed on Lake Eppalock as a little boy. A 12-year-old girl had lost her life in a water skiing accident because of a frayed towrope and a faulty harness buckle. He goaded us into action by imploring us to follow Steve's example and thoroughly check all equipment before venturing into anything.

By humanising basic nuts-and-bolts information with a story you'll bring it to life and not only make it more relevant to your listeners, you'll goad them into action!

> **Tip:** You don't have to tell a story for every single point you wish to make, as long as real people and examples feature somewhere in your talk. Add a touch of 'how to' advice as well as some facts and figures. And it's okay to pick up data and read it if it's complicated.

Agenda-driven presentations

Another objection to this conversational approach is: "Most of my talks are agenda-driven where we're pushed through like sausages in a machine with only a few minutes to get our point across." If you are in this situation, here are two suggestions that could help you.

If your purpose is to *inform* with factual information, you could relive from memory the circumstances that led to the acquisition of this information. On a new biodegradable discovery, a leading scientist once told his esteemed peers:

> When I walked into the laboratory this morning I noticed everyone excitedly milling around the microscope. I thought, *That's strange … What's going on here?* I walked over and Mary Sanders said, "Take a look in here." What I saw astonished me. There before my eyes was the culmination of four years of research. We'd finally done it!

He then stated the facts and the possible paths along which this exciting discovery could take them.

If your purpose is to *persuade*, all the more reason to package what you have to say in something that appeals to all the senses! Margaret

discovered the importance of this. With only eight minutes to persuade a tight-fisted government body to give extra funds for Family
Care, she appealed to the hearts and minds of her listeners with a
story.

After thanking them for the opportunity to speak, Margaret
wasted no time in having them experience the hardship for themselves. Reliving an actual incident from memory, she took them
into a home full of despair where they saw a young mother seated
at the table, head in her hands and bills piled high around her. An
unchanged baby was screaming on the floor, a toddler was clamour-
ing for attention and the sink was full of dirty dishes. What's more,
there wasn't a scrap of food in the house. This young mother was at
her wits' end.

She went on to say that thanks to Family Care, three months
down the track there was food in the fridge, the kids were clean and
new agreements had been negotiated with her creditors. But most
importantly, this young mother now believed there was hope. This,
Margaret explained, was why Family Care was so important. The
dedicated support network provided by highly qualified people was
what broken families like this so desperately needed. And without
government help, none of this would have been possible. Margaret
got her money.

Facing a hostile audience

One of your worries might be: "How do you have a friendly conversation with a room full of people hell-bent on giving you a hard
time?" Well, there are two things working against you here: you are
pumped with the nervous adrenalin of public speaking fear and your
listeners are spoiling for a fight! You must accept the fact that it's
impossible to persuade every person in your audience that what you
say is right, but you can always strive to be friendly and agreeable
and gain their respect. Let me illustrate how to avoid fanning the

flames of hostility as you try and win them around to your way of thinking.

Persuading unpersuadable people

I once did some work with a group of Department of Conservation and Environment park rangers, who were being heavily criticised by the community as a result of a highly publicised kangaroo cull in a National Park. The kangaroos were being culled because of drought and overgrazing, and were in a bad way. "When we talk to groups they see us as nothing more than callous killers," they complained. "You can feel their hostility ... "

If, as with these park rangers, your subject is a hot potato, it's important not to blatantly push your own barrow. Genuinely try to see things from your listeners' point of view. Go out of your way to start with something you all agree on, even if it takes some digging to uncover this common ground. This will help you win their trust and respect. The common ground between these rangers and this audience was the wellbeing of these kangaroos and the desire to protect them.

When dealing with a hostile audience, ask yourself the following questions:

- Why are these people so negative and uncooperative?

- What are some of the difficulties they have in understanding your actions or point of view?

- What common ground do you have with these listeners?

Put yourself in their shoes and address these questions from their point of view. Look for reasons behind their feelings and address these reasons in a friendly, non-aggressive tone. You may not win them all over, but you'll run a better chance of gaining their respect for the duration of your talk.

One possibility for establishing a cooperative environment for these rangers could be to start with a real story of kangaroo overpopulation in a national park and the developing disaster for the park as a whole. This could then be used as a running theme to refer back to in justifying their actions in the best interests of the kangaroos and the health of the park.

Tip: Keep your cool and think 'friendly conversation' even when the heat is on. If your audience senses you're not looking for a fight they'll probably be fair-minded too and listen to your point of view.

These park rangers no longer take audience hostility as a personal affront. They now understand they symbolise something their audiences dislike, and that these types of challenges, along with the good things, often come with the job. Now when confronted by an emotional audience, they respond to the situation rather than go on the attack. "After all", I told them, "you're genuinely doing what you believe is best for the kangaroos. And this is the message you must focus on."

Let's summarise all this with the following thoughts:

1. *They are not attacking you personally.* Whatever is said in an emotionally-charged way is fuelled by all sorts of things, including misunderstandings. They are not having a go at you personally, they are having a go at ideas and actions they don't agree with. A friendly demeanour in what you say will help defuse the situation and create an atmosphere of open-mindedness and respect.

2. *Start by thanking everyone for giving up their precious time in being there.* This disarms them somewhat for they probably didn't expect words of gratitude to be the first thing you say.

3. *Acknowledge the elephant in the room.* Now go on to 'tell it as it is' by saying something like: "With regard to [state the issue under

discussion] many of you have genuine emotions and grievances you'd probably like to vent right now in search of answers … and this is fine for it's our job to listen to what you have to say."

4. *Appeal to their nobler motives and sense of fair play.* Now follow with: "What I ask is that before addressing your specific questions, you kindly do us the courtesy of listening to what we have to say on the situation and why we plan to [explain action] … there'll be plenty of time for your questions at the end … Does that seem fair enough?" In response to this question any reasonable person would acknowledge that this proposition is indeed 'fair' and find themselves nodding in agreement.

You have now created an atmosphere of respect in which to proceed with your presentation. In so doing you won't create a room full of people who think you are absolutely wonderful, but in an atmosphere of respect rather than antagonism you'll have more chance of shifting thinking to a more conciliatory point of view.

And finally, it's essential you follow up on your promise of giving them ample time for their questions. You'll probably find that many of their grievances have already been answered in your presentation!

Tip: Use lots of 'we' statements. No-one likes to feel they're being lorded over. 'We' statements foster friendly communication and put you in the boat with them. 'You' statements can make people feel as if they're being lectured at.

Delivering a paper

People often ask me how this conversational approach could possibly apply to delivering an academic paper. "How long has it taken you to put this information together?" I ask them. Their responses vary from six days to six months. "And how long have you got to deliver it?" "About twenty minutes" is the usual reply. And of course they fall for the trap of trying to cover the whole paper in this short space of time. If you plan to read your paper to your audience, why not spare them being bored to tears and send them a copy? The fact is audiences don't read, they listen.

Here's a different tack you can take to add a human dimension to the delivery of a paper and keep people interested. Acknowledge the challenge of writing your paper, and state your conclusions. Then say something like:

> In the limited time at our disposal, I'd like to share some of the trials, tribulations and surprises that made this paper such a challenging project. You'll all receive a copy to study the finer details in your own time.

Then, referring to your list of five or so key ideas, all you have to do is relive a few of these trials, tribulations and surprises from memory to highlight some of the major points of your paper. Later, as they study your research and findings, these human stories and anecdotes will enrich their understanding of your work.

And don't think, "But they'll never read it!" If you get them interested during your talk, they'll read it as soon as they can get their hands on it!

Tip: Prior to you getting up to speak, always keep a pen and pad handy to jot down things of interest that occur around you. By referring to individuals and 'happenings' in the room your listeners will perceive your talk as 'of the moment' and relevant to them.

Chapter 3 Key points

- Think of any talk you give as a friendly conversation rather than a formal speech.

- Audiences don't read, they listen. When delivering a paper, share some of the trials, tribulations and surprises from memory that brought you to your conclusions. People can later read the paper in detail themselves.

- Accept the initial rush of adrenalin and excitement we all face with any challenge as normal. The secret is to quickly channel this pressure to the audience by asking them a question.

- Body language is a spontaneous and intuitive expression of what you are saying. So don't stage things, just let it happen.

- If you believe you are having a two-way conversation with your audience, they will believe it too! You'll see a sea of nodding heads in response to a question like: "Has anyone ever experienced anything like this before?"

Monitoring your progress Exercise 4

Your answers to these questions will not be worded the same as the answers in the Answer Key on page 197, but your underlying ideas should be about the same. Comparing your answers right away helps you learn.

1. When next you are asked to speak in public, where will your main focus be and what *approach* will you take?

2. Imagine you have been invited to speak at a local community club on a topic that interests you. List three ways you might be able to learn more about your audience to be able to relate to these people better.

3. What are the three main characteristics that intuitively 'happen' in everyday conversation and activate our sensory hot buttons? Why will you include these characteristics somewhere in every talk you'll ever give from this point onwards?

4. Among your business or professional colleagues, there is undoubtedly someone who stands out above the rest as an effective speaker. What are you going to do now, by way of self-improvement, when you are in the presence of this person?

5. Suppose you are a young salesperson attending an informal party made up of people you know and people you don't know. After a while, you notice a man standing by himself to the side, you walk over, introduce yourself and quickly fall into friendly conversation. Unbeknown to you he's in the market for a new sales manager. As you speak he thinks, "Here's a well-groomed, confident young person. Just the person I want on my team! I'm going to watch this person." What is his ultimate impression of you as an all-round communicator when you later step forward and 'say a few words' on behalf of the host to generous acclaim? What leadership qualities does he see in your communicating confidence?

Check your answers and learn!

CHAPTER 4

Removing common stumbling blocks

Now that you recognise your own self-worth and understand the simple secrets of connecting with people on a personal level, let's deal with some common stumbling blocks that may still be in your way.

Like those destructive labels of negative self-worth we dealt with in chapter 2, public speaking stumbling blocks can creep up on us and take hold in much the same innocuous way. All it takes is some critical comment on your public speaking effectiveness by a well-meaning friend or colleague to set a negative train of thought in place that can affect you for years. If this has happened to you let's ensure we decisively deal with it in this chapter.

What do I do with my hands?

A senior engineer for a large public utility once asked me for help. "I have to give a presentation to a large oil company on a deal that's worth 30 million dollars!" he said. "And my biggest problem is: what do I do with my hands?" Now if this wasn't so tragic it would have been funny. But it was very real to him for he'd lived with this debilitating problem for more than 30 years.

I cured this man forever with my simple response. Here's what I said: "Ian … If I were to direct you to keep your hands by your side to prevent them from waving around and being 'distracting', then get you to go about your day communicating with your family, your friends and your clients without moving them, do you think you'd be comfortable and effective?"

He laughed at the absurdity of this suggestion. I then said: "Well, with your presentation to the oil company, I want you to concentrate 100 per cent on how your proposal is going to benefit these people and save them time and money. And, if in the middle of your talk you find your hand pensively resting on your cheek or scratching the top of your head as you ponder an item, let it! If you discover your hands intuitively mirroring your passion for the project, leave them to do what comes naturally! After all, when you're communicating with these very same people in your office on a one-to-one basis you don't give your hands a second's thought."

Ian wrote me a letter six weeks later to share two items of exciting news: not only did they win the contract, he hadn't given his hands a moment's thought since!

Talking too fast

I once invited an audience to share some of the things that prevent us from speaking with confidence before groups. One lady put her hand up and said, "I talk too fast."

I asked the audience, "Who can relate to that?" Many hands went up.

I then asked her, "Who says you talk too fast?"

She hesitated. "People."

"Which people?" I persisted.

"Everyone. It's always been that way."

I then explained that if you are fearful of speaking before groups with all the wrong things inside your head there's a good chance you'll race through what you have to say just to 'get it over and done with'. Adrenaline can cause us to talk fast, so with your opening, deliberately slow it down. Some people ask, "How do you do that?" And I say, "Simple. Consciously – slow – it – down, especially the first words your listeners hear." The audience won't even notice you're doing this and it will look perfectly normal to them. Talking quickly from beginning to end without pausing for breath is not the way things normally go. Everyday situations govern this, for there are times when you slow right down – it depends on where you are, who you are with, and what you are trying to say. Think of what you are saying to each audience in the same way.

I then went on to cite some of these examples that require a more thoughtful, slower way of conversing. Could be we're with someone who has just lost a loved one; someone who is ill and not thinking straight; someone who hasn't a fluent grasp of our language; or simply admiring something of great beauty such as the sun setting over the ocean. On the other hand, you could be reliving those last exciting moments of a nail-biting football match where either team could have won. I guarantee that your expression would be mirroring the fast pace of the action. But even in this context your speaking pace could change: "In the midst of all the jubilation a couple beside me silently wept for their beloved team who had fought so bravely but come up short." I then tied all this back to my listeners by imploring them to just let it happen, and interpret their stories in exactly the same way with their current audience in mind. Not forgetting that by setting central thoughts in place in a slow, measured way with your opening, you have the advantage of putting everyone at ease and creating interest.

At the end of my talk the lady who had initially said she talked too fast came over and said, "I'd like to thank you. I now know where it all started." She then told me that as a little girl her mother would consistently chide her for hurrying through her church reading each Sunday. "Without fail, every Sunday I'd hear those words: 'slow down, you're reading too fast'. By the time I was a teenager the 'fact' that I spoke too fast was a permanent part of my thinking and I've lived with it ever since."

Before walking away she reached out and touched me on the arm: "But I'm fine now and I thank you for that."

So please, avoid using bland sweeping statements that degrade your capabilities. Accept the fact that we all talk fast – and slow – according to the time, place and situation in which we find ourselves. Make this understanding a permanent part of your thinking, but know it's always best to begin your talk in a slow, measured way to help set the scene, get their attention … and take the pressure off you!

A haunting experience

There are defining incidents – such as my awful Tasmanian experience that can haunt us for years and set up habit patterns of speaking failure that become a recurring, self-fulfilling prophesy. Every time we feel threatened with a similar situation it creeps into our consciousness to remind us of the trauma that inevitably lies ahead and just how inadequate we are. So we've got to do something about this negative state of mind.

Graham Skinner had always dreaded reading out loud in primary school. In fact, he managed to avoid doing anything in front of people right up to year 10 in secondary school, but this particular day there was no getting out of it. He had to deliver a talk. Absolute panic took hold of him. The mere thought of having to stand in front of his entire year level terrified him. He told me that each night after that he'd lie awake in a cold sweat hoping it would just go away.

The night before his talk he realised he could avoid it no more. He sat down at the kitchen table and picked the smallest snippet he could find in the newspaper that would be the basis of his talk, stared at it long and hard, and then put it in his trouser pocket. This was the extent of his preparation. He didn't sleep at all that night. He remembers the next morning as a blur, that piece of paper still burning in his pocket, a constant reminder of the fate that awaited him. "As I sat in the front row I was shivering all over and just wanted to be somewhere else," he told me later. He doesn't remember much after that ... walking out to a sea of faces, feeling faint, and grabbing hold of the lectern for support. Though what did ring in his ears for years were the howls of uncontrollable laughter from that merciless crowd as he staggered off stage without a word.

The pain and humiliation of this experience had etched itself so deeply within him that it ran his life. This was now the one and only benchmark against which he constantly measured himself. Yet in one session I got Graham to recognise the experience for what it was – a task far beyond him without the necessary coaching and encouragement to be a success. It would have happened to anyone in the same situation with the same unprepared state of mind. It simply wasn't his fault, so why should he let inadequate guidance and preparation brand him a hopeless public speaker for the rest of his life! Blame rested entirely with the school for throwing this unprepared lad to the wolves without the adequate training and preparation.

I reminded him that he was no longer that frightened little boy. He had travelled the world and now managed a successful business. Graham was faced with a stark choice: stay on the fearful path he'd been travelling for so long or start walking a new one and see himself in a different light. Based on the successful talks he'd given in our workshop, Graham chose to redefine himself and walk the new one. He now measures himself against the 'friendly' habit patterns of speaking success he now enjoys because of the lessons learned in this approach, instead of the destructive ones he experienced 20 years before because of inadequate guidance! There comes a time when we must break imprisoning moulds of the past and set ourselves free from the pain of circumstance and events beyond our control, for as we grow, our values, perceptions and understandings are constantly changing. And, if we allow ourselves, we can learn from painful experiences and move on to new and exciting things … Hey, we all have a 'bad hair day' now and again. But we mustn't let them run our lives.

Some years ago I tentatively gave my first Rotary Club talk with the pretentious title 'The Getting of Wisdom.' It was a woeful effort. No matter how hard I tried, I struggled to hold the attention of that 100-strong audience. The generous applause at the end was because I'd cut my talk short. I couldn't get out of there quickly enough.

But I didn't chuck in the towel. I persevered. Six years later, I found myself doing a keynote talk for the National Speakers Association of Australia (now Professional Speakers Australia). At the end of my presentation a man walked up to me and said: "About six years ago I saw you give a talk at a Rotary Club that would have to be one of the worst talks I've ever seen in my life. Tonight would have to be one of the best. I thought you'd be interested to know that."

So you see, we can move on from a painful experience and establish new positive benchmarks against which to measure ourselves. So don't let one bad experience be your personal 'brand' to haunt you for the rest of your life.

Finding the 'right' words

I was once watching a man speak in the final of a very prestigious public speaking competition when he suddenly went white and his face began to quiver. "I'm sorry," he mumbled, "I can't find the right word." He desperately tried to go on, but couldn't. We all felt for him as he made his way back to his seat, knowing that he'd blown it. If only he had known, there's no such thing as a concrete set of 'right words' when verbally expressing ourselves in public. So talk to the right *ideas* ... thoughts and stories that unfold in a predetermined sequence yet come across as spontaneous and natural.

The spoken word is totally different to the written word. One is carefully contrived, the other is completely unfettered. This is why politicians in the main are so boring – they're shackled to the written word. Their speech writers write things on paper that often do little to engage and inspire when delivered. Your talk must be a dynamic, living thing, able to reflect the mood of the moment. Your words should come naturally as you share the intoxicating essence of an idea as they indeed do in everyday situations. Sometimes they're not even grammatically correct. Concentrate more on connecting with people using ideas and examples they can relate to rather than trying to impress them with the 'right' words. When you speak in public, this fear of finding the right word should no longer be a part of your thinking. Remember, audiences don't read – they listen!

Going blank

"The human brain starts working the moment you are born, and never stops until you stand up to speak in public," said Sir George Jessel.

We can laugh at this, but many people live in mortal fear of losing the plot or going blank during their presentation. Making reams of detailed, small-print notes, however, is not the way to overcome the problem. First they're hard to read, then, what if you drop them or they get mixed up?

Here's a fact. We live in an impromptu world. Every day of your life you effectively communicate with friends, family, and colleagues by reacting to key ideas and stimuli. You say something, they respond to it. The words just flow as you relive a particular story from memory, or you give a spontaneous demonstration for a minute or two of what you mean. No-one says, "Just a minute, let me refer to what I've got written here." It just happens. What you say is stimulated by key ideas. In contrast, detailed notes confine us to a narrow range of expression. In a public speaking situation, the secret is to have your key ideas close at hand so you can't lose your way. These could be nearby key words or phrases, charts, objects or pictures – each triggering an example to illustrate what you mean … in effect you're duplicating the stimuli of everyday conversation.

Occasionally I ask my audiences, "Is it normal for people to lose their train of thought in everyday situations … for example, 'I've forgotten what I was going to say', 'Where did I put my pen?', or, 'It's on the tip of my tongue.'" They nod at the obvious naturalness of this. I then ask: "Would it be normal to assume that these same people might lose their train of thought when speaking before a group of people?" They find themselves nodding at the obvious naturalness of this also.

When I'm in front of people and lose my train of thought because someone asks me a question or some wag says something funny, I'm no longer overwhelmed with the panic of losing my way and getting lost. When things have settled down and I'm ready to get back on track, I have those friendly mental joggers laid out in sequence nearby to tell me where I am at a glance and what to talk about next. Let's explore this …

When this inevitably happens, the first thing to remember is not to flag the fact that you don't know where you are with a negative comment like, "I'm sorry, I've lost my way." It looks bad. I've learned to turn a loss of thought into a powerful dramatic pause and that people appreciate time to reflect on what's been said. If you're in control of the situation, thoughts will continue to reverberate in people's minds even though the words have stopped. Casually walk over and look at your list of key ideas as if it's the most natural thing in the world. Be extra cool, and muse out loud as you go with something like, "Interesting isn't it … " You'll see top speakers use these little musings to stimulate reflection as they gather their thoughts in order to lead into their next main idea. You can do the same to guide the thoughts of your listeners.

And then there's the glass of water. It looks perfectly normal for you to have a sip of water during a presentation, but right beside the glass are your notes, a short list of key words (printed in large type) or symbols that tell you where you are at a glance. If you get stuck, have a sip of water, glance at your notes, then giving the impression that you're in total control and not at all flustered, link back to where you left off. It comes across very naturally.

If you're giving an informative demonstration or talk, any items you have set out before you will help guide you. No matter what happens, a quick glance at the screen or objects laid out before you will show you precisely where you are and you'll be able to move on to your next story or example with ease. Remember it's all very safe, for you laid these life-saving mental joggers out yourself.

A lady in one of my workshops was still not convinced that a set of strategically placed mental joggers would cure her of her long-held fear of going blank. During the course of the program, I discovered that she was a passionate collector of old bottles, and that each one of these bottles had a fascinating story behind it. Cathy knew these stories well and was eager to share them with anyone who showed an interest. I asked Cathy to stand four of these bottles up in a box out of view of the audience, not in any particular order. She began her talk with the words:

> The household discards of today often become the lost voices
> of the past. Luckily, bottles don't deteriorate with time and
> tell us much about those who came before us.

She then put her hand in the box and pulled out a bottle at random, a little hand-made inkbottle. "Now this is interesting … " she began. Then with all the naturalness in the world, Cathy told the bottle's story from memory.

She got us to imagine an early Victorian gold miner writing a letter to a loved one by flickering candle light in his rudimentary tent with ink from this very bottle! And when the bottle was empty he simply threw it out onto the diggings to be discovered by us many years later. Cathy said that thousands of these little bottles have been found on the gold fields. She then picked up another bottle at random, smiled as its meaning came to mind, and confidently began her next story. Cathy says this one talk convinced her of the power of strategically placed mental signposts and permanently rid her of her fear of going blank.

Your notes, therefore, should be nothing more than a box of 'bottles' placed where you can see them. So no matter what the cause of a loss of thought, a quick glance at your next 'bottle' will tell you precisely where you are and what to say from there. It really is that easy.

> **Tip:** Notice how Cathy did not hand these fascinating bottles around for people to look at during her talk. She stayed in control by inviting her listeners to look at them afterwards. And the same thing applies to handouts. A comment such as: "I have some interesting notes for everyone … please take a yellow sheet on the way out," will avoid unwanted distractions. I once saw a speaker hand a person in the front row a brochure as an illustration of what he was saying. For the duration of his talk that brochure snaked its way from row to row stimulating lively discussion as it went! It completely disrupted the talk.

Another strategy to ensure you don't lose your way is the use of memory pegs, the mental version of Cathy's box of bottles. Simply reduce each of your main ideas to a vivid mental picture that denotes a key aspect of your talk. The more absurd and colourful it is, the easier it is to remember. For example, Cathy's first picture could be an early gold miner sitting in his rudimentary tent writing by flickering candlelight, stimulating the 'ink bottle' story. The next picture could be blood-red tomato sauce oozing out of a hand-made sauce bottle all over a corner of the miner's calico tent (each new image must be physically linked to the preceding picture). This could lead into a story on how the bottle was made and who made the sauce that filled it. And on it goes ...

The secret is to reflect a moment as you visualise the physical link with the last picture, then launch into your next idea. Spend one session quietly locking your memory pegs in place, and then use them as your mental joggers as you rehearse. (You'll learn more about rehearsing later.) Five or six of these pictures are usually enough. Most of my keynote presentations are delivered in this way. But for now probably the easiest way is to refer to your 'box of bottles'.

Of course, the added benefit of turning a train-of-thought loss into a powerful communicating tool is that you have one less thing to lie awake at night worrying about.

> **Tip:** You may choose to use an acronym, a real or imaginary word where each letter triggers your next main idea. Your acronym could be written down, projected on a screen, or kept in your head.

Correct English

Another question I'm often asked is, "What do I feel about the use of correct English in being an effective communicator?" In response I relate the story of Michael.

Now Michael once stood up in one of my workshops to share his thoughts on the unemployed. I can see him now ... tall, distinguished, with well-groomed silver hair. He was extremely articulate, his diction was perfect and he had one of those voices that pleasantly resonates around the room.

For about five minutes this well-spoken man quoted this survey and that ... He cited the latest unemployment statistics and a few other facts and figures that came to mind. He concluded with his general thoughts on the subject.

Do you know what I remember about that talk? That's right, the way he looked and his voice. I wasn't inspired or motivated to remember the key points of what he had said. When he sat down I asked, "Michael, do you know any unemployed people?"

He thought for a moment: "As a matter of fact I do."

"Would you mind coming back and telling us about them."

He thoughtfully told of a couple he knew in rural Victoria who were both schoolteachers and who were made redundant because of government cutbacks in education. This put an immense strain on their relationship for they could no longer pay their bills or treat their kids to the simple things that had given them so much joy. They struggled on as best they could for a year or so with a bit of casual work here and there. Finally, unable to take any more, they went their separate ways. At this point Michael thought deeply, then with a voice full of emotion said: "And I lost two dear friends." He walked back to his seat without another word, leaving these thoughts reverberating in the minds of his listeners.

I looked at the audience and asked: "Which one of those talks resonated with you the most?"

So you see technically correct English, wonderful diction and a vast vocabulary are certainly an asset, but they have little to do with communicating on a human level. Either you connect with your listeners or you don't. The key is to bring general observations and sterile facts and figures to life with examples that people can easily relate to.

English fluency

In another of my groups, Nobyuko, a senior executive in a large Japanese organisation, was absolutely terrified that he might be asked to talk in front of his Australian peers. He begged me to bypass him, as his command of English was somewhat limited. I pulled him aside and learned that as he travelled the world he missed his family terribly. I said to him, "Could you share a little of how you feel about your family with us?"

In halting English he began to speak … and as his story unfolded you could have heard a pin drop. Few people in that audience will ever forget the picture of Nobyuko's little boy running up to give his dad a big hug on his return, and this has little to do with Nobyuko's command over the English language. It's universal.

Nobyuko now has a new understanding of himself, his Japanese turn-of-phrase and his accent. He accepts these things as a stamp of his uniqueness for they help him connect on a human level and endear him to his listeners. And as his mastery of English improves and he learns more about our culture, he'll continue to grow in confidence but still be happy with who he is.

And it's a similar story for Italian immigrant Olga Giuliani, author of the inspirational book *The Little Oak Tree*. I've seen Olga hold an audience in the palm of her hand for an hour speaking the English she learned from the 10 kids she had to bring up in Australia single-handedly as a deserted mother: the fun, the drama, the trials and tribulations all delivered in her endearing turn-of-phrase and her limited vocabulary.

The lesson for us here is, true communication runs far deeper than mere words and fluency of tongue.

Cultural differences

And likewise with cultural differences. The thing that was holding Raman Powandra back as a confident communicator was his total unease in the presence of his Australian superiors. The thing that really perplexed him was that he was the complete opposite when he was with his own subordinates for there he had none of these uneasy feelings of deference. We soon discovered why. For the first 20 years of his life in his native India, respect for one's elders meant total deference and subservience for the young Raman. He clearly remembered his first day at university as the day his father finally permitted him to stand in his presence.

Now compared to our egalitarian society and the easy-going nature of Australians, Raman found the backslapping familiarity of boss with subordinate hard to fathom and completely alien to his thinking, so when in the presence of those above him he felt completely out of his depth and uncomfortable. Once I got him to accept that this is the natural order of things in Australia, that this is our culture, our way of fitting in and being accepted, his uneasy feelings of speaking up in high-powered meetings vanished. Now Raman comfortably moves between cultures communicating with ease. He defers to those above him when it's the cultural thing to do, and communicates with Australians on equal terms whatever their station in life. Raman discovered that his biggest problem had been one of cultural misunderstanding. And in understanding our culture he learned to understand himself and how to communicate more effectively with all levels of society.

"Ums" and "ahs"

Then there is the chap who confessed to having a chronic problem with "ums" and "ahs" (mind you, as he was speaking to me I didn't detect it). I said to him, "How long have you been aware of this problem?"

He shrugged. "As long as I can remember."

After talking to him for a while, I finally nailed something down. At university a well-meaning friend studying speech therapy had criticised his performance after a nerve-wracking experience in a tutorial.

"I counted at least 20 'ums' and 'ahs'," his friend had said. "You'll have to do something about that ... You've got a real problem." The destructive seed was sown. From then on he indeed did have a problem. And as the years went by it became worse, to the point where it became part of his thinking and was an undeniable fact.

If an occasional "um" or "ah" slips out, or you trip over your tongue, if you don't worry about it your listeners won't either! It shows that you're a real human being and talk just like them. Simply keep going and focus on the message you want to get across. I get paid to speak, and I can tell you that I've yet to give a perfect speech in all the years I've been doing it, for it's all the little foibles in the way I speak that make me interesting!

> **Tip:** Beware of the old adage "practise makes perfect". For one thing the search for perfection is fraught with danger for there is no such thing as a 'perfect' public speaker, only interesting, engaging ones. And what if you're practising the wrong things with the wrong voice inside your head? That just reinforces the negatives and makes things worse! Audiences aren't looking for perfection, they're looking for connection.

Perhaps the worst models for us to follow are those pillars of perfect speech, television newsreaders. They might look perfect and sound perfect but they have been polished clean with special voice training. All the glitches have been ironed out and everything they say is read from a teleprompter. Speaking to a camera in an isolated newsroom has little in common with the dynamics of interacting with a live audience.

But to make you feel better, here's how to remedy "umming" and "ahhing" between sentences if you feel it really is a problem. Simply close your mouth between main thoughts. It's that simple. An "um" or an "ah" is nothing more than you exhaling air and thinking out loud as you mentally transfer to your next thought.

Going red

In one of my workshops a lady once began a talk with, "I guess you all notice I'm going red."

To be honest we hadn't really thought about it but as we'd all been invited to notice we all craned forward and thought, *Well, not really … but now that you mention it.* And of course she went redder and redder and did her best to somehow get by. It was painful to see her trying to hide her embarrassment. All she wanted to do was get her talk over and done with and sit down.

Christine did not have some innate problem of uncontrollable blushing. She is a highly qualified pediatric nurse, very competent in her job dealing with people in sensitive and high-pressure situations. Yet for as long as she could remember she'd had this problem of blushing whenever she was the centre of attention. Everyone knew about it and everyone talked about it. Her mum and dad, her relatives, her classmates, and even her teacher! So here she was, a grown-up person in this class openly proclaiming this embarrassing affliction to us all. Conditioned to think this way all her life, she had talked herself into going red whenever she did anything in public, and she inevitably lived up to her expectations – going red had become a self-fulfilling prophecy. She believed she'd go red, so she went red. This was simply how things were.

During our break, I took her aside and made her promise that she'd never again put herself down in public with a self-effacing apology and never again mention going red when speaking before groups. Not even to herself! I told her that at times we all go red when we feel embarrassed … it's part of being a human being. But why flag it every time we open our mouth? The following week I got her to do a re-run of her talk, 'Stress in the Unborn Child' … with the proviso of no mention of her going red! The results were amazing.

Christine grabbed our attention with: "Two weeks ago a distressed young mother-to-be was wheeled into emergency in premature labour … One look at our equipment told us that this was serious, with both the mother's and baby's lives in immediate jeopardy. With only minutes to spare we raced her into theatre!" We listened in rapt attention as we experienced her team going into action and the incredible things modern technology can do to monitor stress in the unborn child and deal with this type of emergency.

The baby and mother were both saved, but it was touch and go. And guess what? As this incredible story unfolded the possibility of Christine going red was the farthest thing from our minds!

In fact, this talk had such a profound effect on her that she's never mentioned going red again – anywhere! If she goes red now it's just a fleeting thing, like it is for the rest of us. As a result, her long-held problem of going red no longer bothers her and she now communicates with confidence, for there are more important issues to worry about.

Fear of a large audience

Whenever I ask a group, "Who feels uneasy in front of a large audience?" a sea of hands go up. Well, if you're one of these people you don't have to live with this fear any more either. Let's see why.

Imagine this – you're on the way to a function to hear someone speak on a favourite topic of yours. You've looked forward to this event for weeks ... you've even convinced a number of close friends to come along, and you're excited about it! Now, do you think you'd be saying to yourself, "Tonight I'm going to be part of an unfriendly mob hell-bent on destroying the reputation of the speaker? I hope we reduce this person to a quivering wreck so they run off the platform in tears and never speak again!"

The notion is so silly it's laughable. Yet this is exactly what we have been conditioned to expect – large audiences who are reeking with malevolent intent and have nothing else on their minds but our humiliation. But you know the real truth. You've been a part of a large audience many times before. The fact is you're just sitting there as an individual hoping your precious time is not going to be wasted. You're looking forward to being entertained, informed, persuaded and inspired. You're actually willing the speaker to stand and confidently deliver!

One lady said, "But they just sit there staring at me."

And I said, "They're not staring at you, they're looking at you waiting for you to speak. What do you want them to do ... all look out the window"? Another guy said, "All I can see is their beady eyes!" I said, "They haven't got beady eyes, they've got normal eyes ... they're the very same people you feel comfortable with in non-threatening social situations."

And please, don't fill your mind with the commonly suggested strategy of imagining everyone sitting there in their underwear. Simply concentrate on these people as friendly human beings and what your message will mean to them.

Looking your listeners in the eye

In another of my seminars a young man began his talk by inviting us to close our eyes and imagine a particular scene. *Nice little strategy to get us mentally involved*, I thought, and let myself be carried away. The problem was that for the entire talk we waited in vain for him to say, "You can open your eyes now." When asked why he hadn't done this he said, "I'm scared of looking people in the eye, and this way I didn't have to worry about it." Another young woman took her glasses off before she got up to speak for the same reason.

And they are not alone. This is just another of those nebulous conditionings we pick up along the way that has us believe that eye contact with members of our audience is inherently scary. Let's eradicate this myth right now as well. Make no mistake, whether it be in a conversational setting or in front of an audience, when we look people in the eye we all feel more comfortable. You know how uneasy you feel when someone is continually glancing at a watch or looking over your shoulder at someone else. Believe me, if you're looking at some imaginary dot on the back wall or pretending your audience is not there they'll feel the same way ... and so will you! When you meet people's eyes and share a thought with them something magic happens. Our eyes are such a powerful communicating tool that the warmth and passion of the moment seems to radiate out and touch everyone else in the room.

People often ask me, "How long do I look at someone?"

And I say, "For as long as is comfortable." There's no need to move your head from side to side to get everyone in like those open-mouthed clowns at Luna Park, or bore people into the ground with a steely stare. Simply look at someone as you would in everyday situations and make your point.

Tip: Welcome being interrupted. You can almost hear some speakers thinking, "Give me a break, please don't interrupt me. Just let me get this over and done with!" Little do they know they'll feel more comfortable when someone calls something out, asks a question or says something funny. These interruptions help your listeners interact with you and your thoughts and contribute in a real way to the overall sharing of ideas. Welcome them. Most important of all, they take the pressure off you and share it with your audience! Now all you need do is pick up on your next bottle!

You don't have to keep looking at an audience non-stop either. Think what you do when talking to friends in casual conversation. In order to allow your mind to access a new thought you find yourself looking away and musing to yourself about the topic at hand: "Ah yes," you say as you catch their eye again, "but that's not all ... You'll never guess what happened next." Then, as this new idea enters your mind you pick up the other person's eyes again with something like, "You know my old boss Bill Smith?" ... And away you go again! You can do the very same thing in front of an audience. It adds a perfectly natural dimension to your speaking as you casually look away at the end of a main idea and reflect for a few seconds as your mental joggers help you segue into your next thought.

So remember, your eyes are an integral part of you as a communicating entity. Use them to put everyone at ease and help people connect with you on a human level.

If something unforeseen happens

If a waiter drops a tray of glasses, or you knock a jug of water over, or the air conditioner breaks down, or the microphone is playing up, don't pretend everything is okay and simply soldier on. Stop and show concern or get someone to fix it.

At the very least, acknowledge the interruption. People understand that things can happen beyond our control. At a well-known hotel in Melbourne, time management guru Daniel Johnson once found himself competing with the deafening thud of a hammering water pipe in a wall at a crucial part of his presentation. He quipped: "People are so excited about the ideas we're sharing in here they're banging on the walls trying to get in!" His audience enjoyed this and Daniel continued with his talk. Ten minutes later it happened again but this time they were in on the joke. They laughed when Daniel wryly observed: "They're determined!"

Tip: If you notice a person nodding off in your audience, change pace by getting everyone to stand and stretch or share an idea with each other. Don't take it as a personal reflection of your communicating ability. For all you know they may have been travelling since the early hours to be there!

A few years back during one of my speaking workshops in a local college, an aerobics class set up camp in the room right next to us. The incessant thump, thump, thump of deafening disco music was very disconcerting for people trying to overcome their fear of speaking before groups. More out of desperation than good management

I said, "This is the sort of interruption that can happen in real-life situations. Let's treat it as a learning experience and focus on the messages we want to get across in spite of the noise." It even became a sort of running joke, all because I'd acknowledged the situation and suggested how we could make the most of it. Luckily the aerobics class finished long before we did!

My audience won't respond to a request or directive

A speaking colleague once said to me, "I'm a bit tentative about asking my audience to turn and share something as part of my talk … What if they won't do it?" I allayed her fears with the following story.

I once spent a few days watching the world go by from the steps of the breathtaking Milan Cathedral in Italy. And what a fascinating experience it was with all the comings and goings as the locals intermingled with the tourists in the town square. But there was one chap who intrigued me no end – the resident photographer. He was nothing to look at really. He was short, rather dumpy and bald. But he did believe in what he was doing!

In cahoots with the local pigeons, he'd descend on unsuspecting tourists strolling across the square. Within seconds he'd have their hands full of corn and be snapping pictures left, right and centre as they laughed nervously with pigeons flapping all over them.

Then with the confident air of someone in complete control of who he is and what he's doing, he'd turn his back on his bemused subjects and beckon them to follow him. Somewhat bewildered, they'd take a few tentative steps, wondering just who this guy was and what it all meant. The pattern was always the same. After about 20 metres he'd turn and enthusiastically motion them to catch up, as if to say, "Hey! What's keeping you!" Invariably they'd follow. Ten minutes later they'd emerge from a little shop at the side of the square, excitedly looking at themselves in the photos they'd just bought! And despite the different nationalities, all this was done in Italian!

Twenty years later I employ the same strategy with my audiences whenever I want them to interact by doing something. A firm but friendly directive to 'share an idea with a partner', 'introduce yourself to someone you don't know', 'form groups of three to see what you come up with', or, 'turn and share one thing you've learned so far' is my version of confidently directing the tourists to 'follow me'. Then, with absolute confidence that they'll carry out my wish, I say a final, "Away you go!". I turn away and take a sip from my glass of water. With me now not taking their attention, there's nothing left for them to do but carry out my request. And, exactly as occurred in that town square all those years ago, they go ahead and do it! It never fails. It never fails because my listeners sense they're in the presence of someone they can trust, someone who really believes in what he's doing.

By the way, my speaking colleague did the same, and with the same results. She now understands that audiences appreciate being led by someone who knows what they're doing so she leads them with confidence!

Tip: Just as audiences appreciate being led into an activity, they also appreciate being told when to stop. There's nothing worse than a group of people left standing or wondering when to finish chatting to the person sitting next to them. A clear "please be seated" or "let's stop here and see what we've come up with" will keep you in control and prevent things from wandering all over the place.

Opening your talk with impact!

People often tell me that those first two minutes of a talk are the most fearful because it's here that they feel the most vulnerable to failure. This is certainly the case if you have no set strategies to engage your listeners so that they sit up and listen.

The first thing to consider is what to do about that deadly combination of your heart racing out of control and your audience sitting there thinking, "Let's check this guy out … " Not the perfect setting for a friendly chat! Well, the rest of this chapter will show you how to take control of this uncomfortable situation in those first few moments so you not only grab their attention, you transfer all the pressure off you and onto them and relax your racing heart so you can settle into an enjoyable conversation that connects with people.

Use the following suggestions to involve your audience and make them believe they're in for something special.

Acknowledge your audience

Ideally you'd have someone to set the scene and introduce you to welcoming applause so you step forward with a fine reputation to live up to, look at the friendly faces of your audience and begin to speak. But if it's one of those situations where you have to introduce yourself it's best to say a few friendly words acknowledging your audience before launching into your prepared 'attention grabbing' opening.

With a group of people who have braved a cold rainy night to attend your talk you could say: "Ladies and gentlemen I do appreciate your efforts in braving such a miserable night to be here … I assure you, you're precious time won't be wasted." These thoughtful words would immediately strike an appreciative chord. *He's considerate*, they'd be thinking. *It is an awful night and it wasn't easy to get out* … With a group of business people who have given up some of their limited lunchtime you could say: "I do thank you for allowing me to encroach on your lunch time and I appreciate the fact that some of you have come across town to be here … I'll be brief and to the point, then I'll be joining you for lunch!" Or you could be a guest speaker at a group you were once part of. Some opening remarks like the following would rekindle pleasant feelings between you and your listeners: "It's great to be back and see you all again … none of you have changed for you all look as young as ever!" These words of acknowledgement will warm your listeners towards you before you even begin.

Even if something momentous has happened it's probably best to clear your listeners' minds and not ignore it. I was at a business seminar the morning the Americans bombed Bagdad in the first Iraq war and everyone was talking about it. The first thing our presenter said was, "The Americans have really pulled the pin this time! … But we've got a task to do today so let's concentrate on that and inform ourselves of what happened later." These things said, you are now ready to hit them with an emotional opening to grab their attention and take the pressure off you!

Ask a question

Here you could open with a statement that everyone can identify with: "Has anyone here ever felt uncomfortable in a room full of strangers, and found yourself thinking: *I wish someone would come and talk to me?* Give them a few seconds to respond, then say: "I'm glad I'm not the only one!"

This sets up an air of agreement between you and your audience. It also brings you to their level as a fallible human being.

Or, "Have you ever wondered why some people can speak effort-lessly before groups while the rest of society find it a real challenge? … Well, tonight we're going to let you in on a couple of secrets on how you can have your share of it too!"

They're now tuned in to what you have to say and are eager to learn!

Involve your audience

Any audience involvement at the beginning of your talk takes the pressure off you and helps set the mood. For example, with a talk on 'customer service excellence' you could invite your entire audience to stand, then sit down in stages if they, or someone they know, has experienced indifference; rudeness; insincerity; or bad service of any kind. Eventually everyone will be seated and focused on the essence of your talk. Notice how general this is so it can't help but get everyone in!

> **Tip:** People don't want to be seen as the odd one out. If you want your listeners to raise their hands in response to a question, raise your hand first (only half way up) as you ask your question. And, as if by magic, many hands will mirror this gesture. It's irresistible. This is an effective way to get people physically involved in your talk and take the pressure off you!

Create mystery

You could start by involving your listeners in a mental picture: "Imagine this: Three people huddled in a flimsy tent in the middle of a raging blizzard ... Suddenly the terrifying crack and rumble of an avalanche echoes through the valley."

At this point the audience doesn't know who these people are, what they're doing there or what fate awaits them. Keep them guessing ...

And likewise with the following:

"Imagine yourself a young wife-to-be in preparation for her marriage to the man of her dreams. She is all excited and thrilled about using her mum's beautiful wedding dress. Her new husband has his own business and she has a job to go to when she moves to Melbourne ... 12 months later she finds herself with a new-born baby, no job, no money, husband in prison, and living in a women's refuge 600km away."

A minute has gone by, the speaker's adrenalin energy has been transferred to her expectant audience and they're on the edge of their seats wondering how all this came to be ...

The 'eavesdrop' method

Like creating a mystery, this opening appeals to our innate curiosity. Have your audience feel they are eavesdropping on some private reverie by beginning in a quiet, reflectful way. You could begin your talk with something like this: "You know it's interesting … every time I hear a magpie warble it reminds me of an incredible experience I once had when my young mother and I were caught on a railway bridge when I was five years old … with the whistle of a train in the distance!"

Curiosity is compelling. Your listeners will find themselves craning forward so as not to miss the rest of the story. What on earth were they doing on the railway bridge anyway? Beginning your talk with a open story of human interest will have them involved in it!

Disturb them

An opening such as, "Do you realise that as you drove here tonight 25 people ran the risk of killing themselves on Victorian roads?" has a lot more impact than saying, "Tonight I'm going to talk to you about road safety."

Hit them with a thought-provoking statement

A speaker once opened a local-government seminar on health services with the following words: "What we learn from history is that we don't learn from history!" The audience of long-suffering ratepayers sat in rapt attention!

Make a big fat claim

"Ladies and gentlemen, you are about to learn the simple, yet powerful secrets of being a panic-free public speaker."

If you begin your talk like this, most people would be eager to know what these simple secrets are. And of course after a big fat claim like that you've got to come up with the goods!

Make a shocking statement

Some years ago a young lady from the Pap Test Registry was about to address a rowdy group of teenage girls at a local high school on the importance of pap smear tests in the fight against cervical cancer. She felt deeply about her message, but her young audience was hell-bent on giving her a hard time. She walked to the front of the room, slammed her folder down on a table, looked them in the eye and said: "Six people in this room will be dead before they reach the age of 30!" They sat in shocked silence.

Dramatise your ideas

I'll never forget the guy who began his talk by flipping a small bag of rice a couple of times in the air as if to weigh it. He threw it to one or two people in the front row for them to get an idea of the weight of it as well. Then, pointing to the small bag in the palm of his hand, he said: "This was about the size of my little boy when he was born eight weeks premature. His little arms and legs barely hung over the edge of my hand ... It broke my heart to see him so helpless covered in all those wires and electrodes."

Fearing the worst, we wanted to know what had happened ...

Drama can also be used to capture attention with a less emotional subject. I once saw a well-dressed speaker walk to the front of the room wearing a pair of goggles and carrying a red velvet cushion with what appeared to be a white billiard ball perched in the middle of it. He gently went down on one knee, picked up a sledgehammer and unceremoniously gave the ball an almighty whack! He took off his goggles, picked up the undamaged ball and calmly said: "Ladies and gentlemen – ceramics, the material of the future." He had our complete attention.

You might not want to be so elaborate. A sheet of paper held up containing the latest figures on your topic, then dropped like a piece of worthless rubbish would dramatically convey your disdain for what was on it and serve as a great opener for your alternate point of view.

Massage their egos

I was once keynote speaker at a conference for professional speakers. And I assure you, standing before the critical eye of my peers was rather daunting. Here was a group of people that probably thought they knew it all. What could I say to them that they hadn't heard before? Here's how I went about it.

My opening words massaged their egos: "Ladies and gentlemen, to gain the collective speaking experience in this room I'd probably have to live several lifetimes ... but I'm sure you'd all agree there is always room for some new insights."

Every head in the room nodded sagely. I had them! Anything I said after that was an 'insight'.

Of course, I then went on to deliver what I had planned anyway and they loved it. When you feel your audience knows more than you do, why not use this marvellous little strategy to win them over? It works every time.

It's all in the title

Get 'em in before they're in! Sometimes the only information a potential audience has of your talk is some notice or ad they've read somewhere. And if the title isn't catchy your words of wisdom could be lost on an empty room.

Australian Marketing Guru Winston Marsh contends that the title is the most important part of the talk. He knows that if he can't persuade people to come and hear him speak he won't be able to help them make more money in their business. He was once invited to speak to a group of retailers on the topic 'Retailing Strategies for Today', and up until that point they'd had little response. Winston took one look at the title and replaced it with 'How to Pack Your Store with Shoppers All Itching to Buy!' As any retailer would want to get in on this information, the place was full!

But the definitive example of just how intoxicating and far-reaching the right title for your talk can be would have to be the story Joan Saxton tells. Joan was the first person to establish a professional speaking bureau in Australia.

Reg Lipson certainly knew how to wow an audience. A marine biologist and general scientist, he specialised in underwater exploration and the breeding habits of fish. With the clever use of images, audience participation and an infectious personality, he'd have his students at the Royal Melbourne Institute of Technology in stitches. Joan immediately recognised Reg's potential as a professional speaker and made him part of her elite stable of speakers. But beyond the lecture theatre the fish in the kettle were of a very different variety. His general topic of 'Underwater Exploration and The Breeding Habits of Fish' didn't motivate anybody. People simply weren't interested.

Something had to be done. When they revised the title to 'Exotica and Erotica of The Deep' the results were nothing short of astonishing. Overnight Reg Lipson was in great demand as a speaker. Intrigued by the title, radio and television personalities clamoured to interview him. One group of female football supporters at a club luncheon eagerly awaited a male stripper! Reg was horrified to learn of this on his arrival in the foyer, but because he knew his subject so well they loved him anyway.

For Reg, this simple title change generated speaking opportunities that were not there before. In a matter of weeks he was booked out a year in advance and continued speaking for many years.

So get people in before they're in with the title of your talk. There's no need to re-invent the wheel. Use other people's marketing dollars for inspiration. Peruse the catchy headings in magazines or website headlines for stimulation. Focus on the heart of what you want to say and an idea will come to you. Interesting headings such as: 'The Fun and Drama of Bringing up Triplets', 'How to Talk Yourself into More Business Than You Can Poke a Stick At!', 'High Adventure in the Dandenong Ranges', or, 'A Postman's Leap of Faith' would all arouse interest and motivate people to come and listen to you.

Call on the great thinkers of the world to back your point of view

Mark Twain once said, "Few things on this earth are harder to put up with than the annoyance of a good example." How true this is, for it's the example that really drives your point home.

You'll notice how I call on influential thinkers for their thoughts and insights throughout this book to add substance to what I'm saying. And you can do the same with your presentations. The right quote can be a powerful opening or ending for your talk. For example, in a presentation titled 'Getting to the Point' you could begin with the words:

> Abraham Lincoln once said, "If you have 60 minutes to make
> a point, take 40 minutes to plan it and 20 minutes to say it."

You can also use quotes to help you plan your talk. Grab a book from the library or surf the net to see what other people have to say about your topic. Use their words of wisdom as seed thoughts and build your talk around them.

Tip: Another sure-fire formula for a talk plan could be to explore both sides of a situation with two opposing examples, then come down on the side of one of them. If you were presenting two extremes, your point of view could be the 'lesser of two evils' or the 'middle way'.

The proof is in the speaking

Julie put all this to the test in front of three hundred boisterous men at the Victoria Racing Club, where she was invited to share a woman's perspective of the racing industry. This formidable audience of hard-nosed race goers terrified her. With nowhere to go she began to

100

speak by asking a general question they all had to agree with. And to her amazement her audience began to nod in agreement and listen. For thirty minutes they became a part of her personal experiences and stories as she led them along her predetermined path related to her opening sentence. When she sat down the appreciative applause was still ringing in her ears. "The main thing I learned that day," she told me later, "was people don't come to focus on sweating palms and knocking knees, they come to hear what you have to say."

* * *

So these soul-destroying notions are precisely that: notions based on faulty thinking. The fear of a large audience is in your head. You should now be able to replace it with an understanding of individual people being on your side and waiting for you to enlighten them with something exciting and new.

But there are always exceptions, for not all audiences are friendly: a politician addressing an audience with an axe to grind, or the boss with the unenviable task of announcing a 'restructuring' program to his uncertain staff. This type of situation was addressed in chapter 3 – 'Facing a Hostile Audience' – and is again explored in chapter 7 – 'Thinking on Your Feet Under Pressure'. But be assured, in 99.9 per cent of cases you'll be talking to people eager to hear what you have to say. Why else would they be there? All you have to do is believe in you having earned the right to be there, and implement the strategies in this book to settle your nerves and engage them!

Chapter 4 Key points

- Accept the fact that we all talk fast – and slow – according to time, place and situation. The same thing applies when speaking before groups. Only here, slow things down a bit and deliberately be a little more measured.

- Your focus should not be on finding the 'right words' when expressing yourself in public. The right ideas and stories are what your audience is after.

- Organise your key ideas and visuals so that you can see them at a glance. If you lose your way these mental joggers will enable you to smoothly move on to your next example with ease.

- Audiences love to be led. A firm but friendly directive from someone who believes in what they are doing will have them respectfully carrying out your wish.

Monitoring your progress Exercise 5

Answer all of the following questions before checking with the Answer Key, page 198 at the back of the book. Since your answer may not be worded exactly the same as the model answer, use your own judgment when marking yourself.

1. Where do the majority of our fears reside and what can we do to get rid of them?

2. What is the difference between technical body language and believable body language?

3. What does talking to the right ideas compared with finding the right words mean?

4. Describe a simple strategy you could use to get back on track should you lose your train of thought.

5. Why are television newsreaders not a good example against which to measure yourself as a speaker?

6. Why is a self-effacing apology an ineffective way of beginning a presentation?

7. Give three reasons why it is so important to make eye contact with people when you speak to them.

Check your answers and learn!

CHAPTER 5

Presentations that sell!

Everything we have looked at so far can be applied to all types of speaking, though there are a few extra ideas you can use when you are giving a presentation to sell a product or service. Keep in mind that it's potentially more profitable – and less time consuming – to establish credibility via video or with a room full of prospective buyers than to try and sell to each person individually.

As we have already established, the most important person to sell yourself to is you, for only when you can honestly relate to yourself and your own journey are you truly free to relate to others and theirs, and when you relate to people you sell. You sell yourself, you sell your services, and you sell your products!

> **Tip:** Become an expert in what it is you sell. Study all aspects of your products and services relentlessly until you know them inside out. Now when you're asked a question or face an objection, you'll be able to give an informed response that clarifies qualities and benefits and engenders trust in you as their agent.

Once your listeners have bought 'you', the best way to get your audience to buy what it is you're selling is to create in them a desire they'll find hard to resist. Remember that people don't buy 'things', they buy feelings and outcomes, and so the examples in your presentation must tap into the emotions of your audience and show them how your product or service will satisfy their desires. They want to know if your product will give them peace of mind; increase their income; make their work easier; give them more time with their family; make them more attractive; engender admiration. In short, your presentation must answer the central question: "How will your product/service help me?"

And how on earth do you achieve this? It's easy. Just follow these four simple steps:

1. Explain to your audience the benefits of what you are selling, and that there are many things to consider when buying a home, a car, insurance, health food or whatever it is you are selling. Then add, "But there are some pitfalls as well."

2. Make them feel uneasy. Disturb them a little. Put them in what I call 'the pit'. You do this with some kind of disaster story that has your listeners thinking, "I'd hate that to be me!" Begin your story with something like this: "Let me tell you about Mrs Johnson ... "Then replay from memory how she missed out on $20,000 because of poor advice, or how she unwittingly ended up in hospital because of a dangerous diet, or how she was stranded overseas with no insurance. Often your listeners

will relate to the example because they've been bitten before or know someone who has and will be very interested in ways of preventing it happening again! At this point they're still uncomfortably in 'the pit'.

3. Throw them a rope. Let them know you're the one person who can pull them out to safety. Do this by reliving from memory another story where you helped someone avoid the sort of disaster that befell Mrs. Johnson. Your stories will do the selling for you because you'll be speaking of the benefits to your listeners. They will also help you connect on a personal level and show your integrity and product knowledge, but most of all they'll sow the seeds of trust because if your audience believes you've helped someone in some way, they will believe you could very well do the same for them.

4. Make yourself available. Don't be in a hurry to get away. Stay after your talk and chat to people. Your purpose here is twofold: to get to know people, and get their business card or email to follow them up. Be sure to write the essence of the conversation on the back of the card or in an app on your phone in point form. Now when you contact them you'll be talking to friends, eliminating the fear of a cold call. A lot of my business relationships are initiated in friendly conversation before or after a presentation.

Use this simple Four-Step Formula in your sales presentations and I guarantee it will have your listeners eager to know more about your product or service.

Breathing life into a boring sales spiel

A young woman once asked me, "How do I prevent a sales spiel on glue I have to give each day from being boring?"

I asked her, "Is the product any good?"

"The product is absolutely fantastic," she said. "It's me that's the problem!"

Anne soon discovered that if she went on believing that her spiel was boring it would go on being boring! She also discovered that a lot of the problem lies in the term 'spiel' itself, which implies an inflexible set of parroted words and thoughts to be rattled off in the vain hope that something good will happen. This approach won't ignite interest in anyone. Sure, you start off learning your set patter, but in time your presentation should give the impression of an immediate conversation that's happening then and there.

Make it a first-time experience

Sammy Davis Junior, hailed as one of the world's greatest entertainers, was once asked why he never got bored singing the same songs over and over again. And Sammy replied, "Whenever I sing an old favourite it's always a first-time experience for both me and my audience." People occasionally ask the same thing of me and my teachings: "Don't you ever get sick of speaking about the same thing all the time?" And I say, "No, because if it's a first-time experience for my listeners, it's a first-time experience for me, and we all grow." The fact is the unique chemistry generated between the speaker and that specific audience can never be duplicated.

I once worked for two years leading camping tours for young people 'in search of the Vikings' around Scandinavia. I found my bag of re-usable stories and one-liners indispensable. I'd trot these out at the appropriate time as we explored the culture and exploits of these intrepid travellers. Far from being bored, my charges loved my stories and quips because they'd never heard them before. And the rapport we created within each group was unique because the chemistry was always different.

Ever-fresh and interesting

And the same principle applies with any set spiel or demonstration, be it on the applications of glue or the exploits of Eric Bloodaxe. Forget trying to parrot your presentation word for word. Keep some pet phrases, but focus on the central ideas and benefits you want to get across. Speaking using key ideas illustrated with interesting stories will ensure your spiel is ever-so-slightly different every time you deliver it, and this slight difference is what keeps your talk fresh and interesting. Be on the lookout for topical asides and comments you can inject into your spiel to help you relate to a situation and your audience of the day. Understand that your listeners aren't the slightest bit interested in how many times you've previously given the talk. They are looking forward to exciting new information they've never heard before. They are keen to learn and genuinely expect you to be interesting. Don't let them down. Demonstrate your enthusiasm for your product and heed the advice of Sammy Davis Junior by making sure every talk you ever give is a 'first-time experience'.

Tip: Get to your presentation early and get to know people. Before a conference started, internationally renowned speaker Daniel Johnson learned all about cat fishing from a delegate everyone knew. When he talked about cat fishing in his presentation it not only brought the house down, it made him an accepted part of the conference. You can also inject spontaneity into your presentation by using information you gleaned from delegates to introduce ideas you were going to talk about anyway: "During the break Mary Smith was saying how audience involvement takes the pressure off the speaker … and she's right! Let's have a look at that." Even more impressive if Mary Smith happens to be the boss!

Give a demonstration

Like a good story, a demonstration of your product or service will stick in your listeners' minds – sometimes for decades! I remember as a young child my mother used to take us kids to Melbourne as a special outing once a year, and one of the special treats was to visit the Coles cafeteria for lunch. To get there we had to walk through the rest of the store, and there was one demonstrator who would catch our attention year after year. I clearly remember he was selling a product called 'Cold Solder' – hardly the sort of thing one would rush out to buy, yet this enthusiastic chap would attract customers around him like bees to a honey pot. Apart from being entertaining and fun to listen to, his demonstration was dramatic. He'd hold up a cooking pot with a hole in it for all to see. Then right before our eyes in a matter of minutes he would fix it with his magical product. He'd then file it, bang it and do all sorts of things with it to prove that it was as good as new. At the end of his presentation people would clamour to purchase his product whether they had a true need for it or not! My mother always bought a tube.

And I was equally sold on the rather staid subject of asphalting roads. An engineer had the formidable task of convincing his listeners just how interesting road making can be. His topic was the uninspiring: 'How Road Makers End Up with a Completely Flat Surface – Even When the Foundation is Uneven'. Before we had a chance to doze off he produced a miniature-working model of a tar-laying machine, and in a very friendly manner, cranked it up and gave us a fascinating demonstration of how it self-levelled as it went along. Now when I come across one of these huge contraptions in operation on our roads I have a fair idea of what it's doing and how it works.

These two examples prove that a demonstration in your presentation can engage, enthuse, enlighten and convince your audience to buy your products and your ideas.

Your listeners will only buy things they understand

I was once listening to a scientist being interviewed on radio about a revolutionary radio-telescope system designed to eavesdrop on the heavens. The concept of the whole thing was mind-boggling. They positioned one radio telescope in outer space, and then linked it to two others on the earth, one in Central America and the other in outback New South Wales. This massive grid could somehow generate a radio wave net three times the circumference of the earth! As I sat there trying to take all this in the scientist said, "It's a bit like me standing in Perth holding a newspaper and you standing in Sydney and being able to read it clearly."

"Wow," I thought. "I can understand that."

Simple everyday comparisons make the unfamiliar familiar, so that people's minds don't wander and they are with you every step of the way. No listener will ever complain because you make things easy for them.

A bamboozled audience won't buy either

Have you ever been part of an audience where the speaker used unfamiliar words and terminology that made it difficult to grasp the full meaning of what was being said? Few people are going to openly admit to their ignorance and shout out, "I haven't a clue what you're saying!" Most will turn off and think about other things. Here's how to ensure that your listeners stay with you and understand precisely what you are saying the first time round.

I was once listening to a presentation on the interpretation of dreams. In one dream the speaker had Pegasus making a dramatic appearance, and from then on she mentioned Pegasus on a number of occasions. Now here's a word that sounds familiar, but did everyone know exactly who or what 'Pegasus' was? Do you know precisely who or what Pegasus is without having to look it up? When I asked the audience this question, only about half of them put their hands up.

The rest of the audience had been left to guess! Most had an idea that it had something to do with ancient Greece, but they couldn't tell you exactly what it was.

We later had a re-run of the same talk. This time the speaker said: "In one of my dreams Pegasus appeared, that magnificent flying horse of Greek mythology ... " At this point I again asked the audience if they knew who or what Pegasus was. Everyone put their hand up.

So unless every single person in your audience uses your terminology as part of their everyday communication, always qualify it. All it needs is a little explanation like: "Then there are the gudgeon pins, the pin that connects the piston of an internal-combustion engine to the little end bearing of the connecting rod." No-one will think you're teaching them something they already know. Those who are familiar with the term will nod knowingly, those that aren't will be grateful for the thoughtful way you helped them save face and expand their minds. Never assume your audience is 100 per cent with you. To convince them that what you're selling is worth buying make sure they clearly understand just who 'Pegasus' is, so that each progressive element of your talk makes sense to them.

Tip: If a specific audience refers to their customers as clients, you call them clients as well. The same applies to terms like 'viewers', 'patients', 'passengers' and 'guests'. Why insult your listeners' intelligence by doggedly sticking to terms that you are more familiar with. The idea is to get people on side and nurture trust and respect – not rub them up the wrong way!

Find the problem before you offer a solution

Quite often a speaker has to contend with an audience mindset of, "Why should we buy from you and not your competitors?" This can be a real challenge, especially if your listeners are happy with the way things are. One way to approach this is to sow the seeds of trust with the purpose of positioning yourself next in line if and when they need a change.

In an introductory presentation to a group of golf links managers, the national sales manager of an international pump organisation decided on a long-term strategy of sowing seeds of goodwill. David told the story of a visit to a renowned golf course where the greens-man complained that because of some glitch, their pumping system had never worked satisfactorily. "The pressure is so erratic the jets of water tend to rut the surface of the green."

"How long has this been going on?"

"At least two years," the greensman lamented.

This was serious. The first thing that came to David's mind was a new pumping system costing $20,000. *But what if it's not the pump?* David wondered … *and they go to all this expense for nothing?*

After half an hour of trouble-shooting, David came across a small overgrown concrete pad. "What's under this?" he inquired.

"I'm not sure. It's always been there."

When they lifted it they found a small control valve designed to regulate the water pressure. Somewhere along the line there had been a breakdown in communications. A simple turn of the valve solved the problem that had bugged this greensman for more than two years.

Here David 'sold' the principle of his company's integrity and honesty rather than pushing an expensive new pumping system as a solution. His listeners could relate to this example and make the comparisons between his company and his competitors. He let them deduce how much better off they'd be with his organisation than they are with their present supplier. And of course he made himself available to cement relationships after his presentation.

Never knock the opposition

There's an old adage in selling that it never pays to throw mud at the opposition because some of it tends to fly back at you and stick!

Being tactful is the key. Under no circumstances make your listeners look stupid or foolish for a decision they made in the past. Use examples of similar organisations to theirs who have made these foolish decisions so they can see the folly of their ways in others and save face! The most tactful way to make our listeners discontented with their current supplier and want to buy from us is to do this indirectly. Talk about the advantages to be gained from using your product or service rather than spending your time knocking the opposition and the deficiencies of the present system. People want to know how this change is going to help them and why they should go to the effort of investing in your product or service. Stories of satisfied customers they can relate to are the key to persuading them to buy!

I made the above point of not badmouthing my competitors in a talk to a group of salespeople with the following example. When I was a home-improvement salesman, my ideas were forever being compared to the somewhat questionable extension 'solutions' of the salesmen who preceded me. The situation was compounded by having to sell a concept of something that didn't exist to people who had little or no idea of what they really wanted.

Then and there I had to create a mental picture that catered for the functional and aesthetic needs of the family before I could sell the project. The trick was to get my prospects mentally enjoying the benefits of their exciting new extension once I had gleaned enough information to decide on a working concept … no easy task! On one occasion a lady nonchalantly proclaimed: "We want a family room here, a doorway over there leading to another bedroom, and an internal laundry here", as if this was all that's needed for a working design.

Instantly I could see that she had been given bad advice. The set-up would afford minimal natural light, be little more than a glorified walkway and be extremely difficult to furnish, but I resisted the temptation to throw a wet blanket over her enthusiastic ideas and blatantly knock the opposition. Instead I asked her how she sees this new space being lived in and furnished? This way she soon discovered the shortcomings of the design she put forward. So I lifted her spirits with some suggestions of my own. "Why not take advantage of all that northern light and the lovely view of your courtyard and the park with full-length windows along this wall?" I suggested. "We could still make this the family room with a doorway over there leading to a bedroom on the southern side of the house. With this layout the living space would be easy to furnish, especially with the sideboard you love so much, and the laundry and all its plumbing could be left where it is."

Warming to the idea, the lady was soon on her feet, gesticulating excitedly as she began rearranging the furniture in her mind. "We could put the lounge suite over here and the television in that corner with the sideboard along the wall," she enthused. The more she moved her furniture around and visualised how her family would live in this redesigned space, the more she sold the concept and its benefits to herself.

Chapter 5 Key points

- Don't be in a hurry to get away. Stay after your talk and get to know people.

- Approach your sales spiel as a first-time experience for both you and your audience. Remember, your listeners are looking forward to exciting information that they have never heard before.

- Disturb your listeners with a disaster story they can relate to (putting them in the pit). Then throw them a rope. Let them know you're the one person who can pull them to safety.

- Use the language of your audience. For example, if they call their customers clients, you call them clients.

Monitoring your progress Exercise 6

To find out how well you'll relate to your listeners and sell yourself first, answer the following questions with a "Yes" or "No". Turn to the Answer Key, page 199 for all the facts.

1. Is it true that passion and enthusiasm are all you need to relate any subject to any audience?

    ☐ YES ☐ NO

2. Will I run the risk of getting too close to my audience if I interact with them on a personal level with little asides?

    ☐ YES ☐ NO

3. If I wish to change the behaviour of certain individuals in my audience, is the use of metaphors a tactful, effective way to go about it?

    ☐ YES ☐ NO

4. If I wish to sell my ideas, my products or myself to my listeners, should I create in them an eager want and then talk in terms of their interests?

    ☐ YES ☐ NO

Check your answers and learn!

CHAPTER 6

Social occasions

One of the saddest things to hear before someone gets up to speak before a group of friends or family is, "I just want to get it out of the way." And of course these are precisely the anxious feelings this person will radiate. The whole speech is a painful ordeal, and the shorter the better! In contrast, have you ever been at a reception or gathering where somebody gives a talk that moves and entertains? Well, here's how to ensure your special talk is a wonderful experience people will remember for years.

You might recall that speakers who have impressed you were certainly in no hurry to get it over and done with. They were fully aware that their listeners did not expect them to be polished professional speakers, but they did expect them to have given some forethought to what they planned to say. These speakers probably did nothing more than share an anecdote or two. They probably preceded these stories by saying how honoured they were to be there to share a heartfelt thought or two on this special occasion, and concluded by inviting everyone to drink to the health, happiness or success of the person of the moment.

For a social occasion, the first thing to do is establish a context. You might marvel that the little girl who kept you sleepless for the first six weeks of her life has grown into the beautiful woman you see before you. "Despite this," you muse, "we've had our moments." At this point the audience is eager for you to share one or two of those 'moments'.

> **Tip:** If you're speaking 'after dinner', make it a rule never to go on after 9pm or you'll be competing with alcohol for attention. Arrange to speak around 8 o'clock when the tables are cleared. Keep your wits about you; save your celebratory drink till after you've finished your talk!

Sharing one of those 'moments'

At a recent wedding reception the father of the bride set up the following story with the words:

> When I look at Belinda sitting here in front of me, so beautiful, so in control, it's hard to believe she's the little girl who used to throw her food all round the kitchen. We've had our moments … This takes me back to an incident when she was about three years old.

Then, from memory, he relived one memorable Easter eve. He had been out shooting rabbits with three of his mates and arrived home towards midnight. As he prepared to skin his share of the hunt on the kitchen sink a sleepy little voice called out from the hallway, "Daddy, has he been yet?"

More concerned with getting the rabbits cleaned than the significance of her words, Joe whisked his little girl up into his arms to show her the nice surprise he had for tomorrow's dinner. At the sight of three dead rabbits laid out on the sink little Belinda dropped to the floor mortified. "I hate you!" she yelled. "You've killed the Easter Bunny!"

As the laughter died down Joe dryly remarked:

> Rabbit was definitely off the menu the following day, and it was no easy task convincing her that the Easter Bunny was very much alive and hopping.

He then looped back to his central point: "Like I said, we've had our moments."

The audience loved it because they could imagine themselves in the story. They loved it because it allowed them to share the feelings of the moment. They were now well and truly primed for more …

> **Tip:** Use the 'loop formula'. State the central idea you wish to make with your example, relive the example from memory, then loop back and state the central idea you flagged at the beginning. In other words: 'Tell them what you're going to say, tell them, then tell them again!'

The right story for the right occasion

In his book *Humorous After Dinner Speaking*, Malcolm Gray tells of the speech he gave at his niece's wedding. He used the story of an attempted Melbourne-to-Adelaide bike ride by the groom when he was 15 years old. (He had gleaned this gem from the groom's mother.) He changed the format slightly from the way it was originally told so that he saved the punch line till last.

After some sincere comments stating how proud he was, Malcolm set the scene with the following words: "I hope your marriage goes better than the time you set out to ride your bike to Adelaide."

He then replayed from memory how the groom and his friend (who happened to be his best man) had enthusiastically set off on their epic journey at 5am loaded down with food and camping gear:

> By lunchtime all the food was gone. At tea time mum received a phone call: "If you happen to be driving in our direction, we need a lift." By midnight you were sound asleep in your own little bed.

Malcolm concluded with these words:

> As I said, I hope your marriage goes better than the time you set out to ride your bike to Adelaide, because Mum's not coming to pick you up tonight!

This is an example of a memorable speech on a social occasion. The secret is to reflect on past experiences and find the right story for the occasion. Ask close friends and relatives for stories you can use. You could then relive from memory how the groom acted strangely the day he proposed; you could relate the day little Sally upstaged the Principal at the school concert; or you could highlight the groom's generosity with the story of his willingness to help you paint the house during his holidays.

Once you determine which stories you are going to use and the specific point each incident will highlight, you'll find they'll begin to grow on you. These stories will become so familiar to you you'll actually look forward to sharing what happened and how you felt at the time with your audience.

You can get inspiration for your stories from the strangest of places.

The speech was in the cupboard

A friend of mine once expressed concern for a speech he had to give at his daughter's 21st birthday party. "I want to get this right," he said.

"I don't want it to be another boring speech. But what do I say?" He was at a complete loss.

After a few pertinent questions I discovered a priceless gem on which to formulate a speech his guests would remember for years. The week before the birth of his daughter, Dominic went out and bought the most expensive bottle of champagne he could lay his hands on. He was determined to make this the toast of all toasts. His plan was to share it with his loved ones and friends the night little Mariana arrived home after her momentous journey into the world.

But it never happened. Things moved so fast he forgot all about it, and this prized bottle of champagne remained unopened in the cupboard for 21 years! As all this unfolded I sat there stunned! "You mean to say that bottle is still in the cupboard – unopened? What a story! There's the essence of your speech."

With a little coaching Dominic soon had an enthusiastic outlook on how things would eventuate on this night that meant so much to him. He'd simply relive this intriguing story he shared with me from memory as the highlight of his speech.

On the night, when he got to the part of proposing the toast, he did so with this unbelievable story that had waited all those years to be told. Then, with great fanfare, he dramatically produced his precious bottle of champagne from its hiding place:

> Friends, 21 years after the birth of our beautiful daughter it's now time to open this precious bottle of champagne and celebrate … it's waited long enough! … and there are plenty of glasses to go round!

Here, Dominic told me, the crowd went berserk! He waited for things to quiet down, and then said:

> With this champagne we drink to the birth of our baby daughter, we drink to all the joy she's given us in the intervening years – and we drink to the 21st birthday of the beautiful young woman we see before us today.

Dominic couldn't believe the emotional reaction to his speech!

He now knows that the secret of an unforgettable speech is to make your points with everyday happenings the audience can relate to. This simple story not only touched and entertained, it was a priceless gift from a loving father to his special daughter.

The secrets of the storytellers

Let's look at a magic three-word formula to make the task even easier. And it's simply this: 'Past, Present, Future'. Storytellers have been aware of this formula for centuries for it's a natural way to tell a story. Who doesn't instantly connect with 'Once upon a time' to 'They lived happily ever after'? This concept takes your listeners on a journey, showing 'How things were then', 'How things are now', and 'How things will be', and the journey along the way. Your audience will feel at home with this natural progression of ideas. The concept 'Past, Present, Future' is the perfect plan for a talk on a social occasion. Storytellers also know that putting yourself in the shoes of the character and uttering their actual words brings your audience into the story rather than have them sitting there as passive observers. Let's look at an example of how this three-step formula works and just how easy it will be for your listeners to enjoy your talk and follow along.

Imagine for a moment that you are the proud parent of your Peter and are preparing an outline of the things you'd like to say at his wedding to his fiancé Kirsty. But before we look at how easy our Past, Present, Future formula fits into this scenario, it's important you first write down your focus sentence, which embodies the precise reason why you're standing up to speak. This will give you guidance in what to say and the order of things. In fact, it should encompass the conclusion of your talk. For example:

The purpose of my talk is to share with my family and friends the anxiousness I felt the first time I met Kirsty, how we've grown to love her and welcome her into our family, and to invite everyone to join us in drinking to Peter and Kirsty's health and happiness.

Now with this 'end in mind' before you, you have clear direction and purpose as you gather your stories and ideas for your talk on this special occasion.

Begin your talk by extending a warm welcome on behalf of both families, and then express how pleased you are to be here to share some thoughts with them. These words will have a calming effect on your listeners and they will immediately warm to you.

Now we're ready for our Past, Present, Future formula:

- *'The Past'*: Simply decide on a relevant story from the past without concern for the words you'll actually use ... be sure to 'tweak' some of the elements for 'special effect', but in the main just relive it. Remember the objective is to create an atmosphere of a friendly chat over the dinner table (and it's okay to do a rough draft first):

I'll never forget the first time I met Kirsty ... I was lazily pruning the roses in the front garden when all hell broke loose. A Darth Vader–like figure roared into the driveway on a very loud 500cc motorbike and pulled up not a metre from my face! I dropped my secateurs and stood there agape. The apparition calmly dismounted, raised its visor and said, "Hi, I'm Kirsty. Is Peter in?"

I thought: "What have I done to deserve this!"

"Yes," I found myself saying ... somewhat in shock, I motioned towards the door ...

You'd then go on to illustrate how wonderful she turned out to be with a couple of examples of her generosity and 'quirky' ways. You could wind up by making the point that first impressions don't always give the full picture of a person.

- *'The Present'*: Comment on the current situation using another example:

> And to see Kirsty sitting here tonight in her beautiful wedding dress compared with that leather-clad entity that scared hell out of me in the driveway is something to behold ... So first impressions can sometimes lead us astray ... Kirsty is now a very welcome addition to our family. Today, for example, she should have been the nervous one, but earlier she was saying to me, "For heavens sake, will you stop running around in circles! Sit down and let me make you a cup of tea." I did what I was told ... Mind you I've been well trained!

This humanising example would highlight the fact that Kirsty is indeed an accepted part of the family.

- *'The Future'*: Simply speculate on an ideal scenario for the future by highlighting some of the cherished dreams they've shared and finish by inviting everyone to join you in a toast:

> Friends, the obvious love Kirsty and Peter have for each other will continue to grow as they go on experiencing life's journey together. I now ask you to charge your glasses and be upstanding as we wish them lots of health, happiness and good fortune for the future.

People will rise to their feet exactly as you asked as you lead them in a toast to the bride and groom. Remember that people love to be led.

One last thing: if you are celebrating for two people, make sure you keep both of them in the picture with a story on each of them.

* * *

So now you have the simple secrets to giving a successful talk on a social occasion. Whether you use two or three stories to highlight human characteristics and qualities with an overall message, or whether you use the magic formula of 'Past, Present, Future', you will make the occasion live in the minds of your listeners for years to come.

Tip: Some venues shine a very strong spotlight on you during your speech so the audience can see you. Don't squint and turn your head away with some off-putting comment like, "Gee that light's strong!" Pretend that everything is normal and look right through it. You'll soon discern familiar faces responding to your message. Remember that it all looks quite normal to the audience. Lights shining directly in your eyes mean your eyes are not shadowed and your audience can see you.

The eulogy

The sombre nature of the gathering at a memorial service can affect speakers in two ways. They can be scared they might touch on something sensitive and hurt mourners' feelings, or they can be afraid they might lose control and break down and cry. Let's address these issues and see how the words you share at a loved one's memorial will touch everyone and be remembered.

Recently I received a call from a business client with an unusual problem: "I've been asked to give the eulogy at a friend's funeral and I'm a little apprehensive about it."

After a few questions I discovered that his friend had said something strangely prophetic to him over coffee two days before he died. "If anything should ever happen to me," he had confided, "will you help Mary and the kids tidy up my affairs and see that they're okay?"

"Sure," Richard said, thinking nothing more of it. Two days later his friend died of a heart attack.

Here was some information he could use in his talk as a platform for other thoughts. "Oh, I couldn't do that," he replied when I suggested it. "It's far too sensitive."

I then led him to understand that reliving this prophetic conversation he'd had with someone they all knew and loved would endear him to his listeners. The story would highlight just how much his friend cared for his family. All he had to do was give a little thought to how to set the story in a sensitive way:

> You know, Joe must have had some premonition of his imminent journey to the beyond ... Two days before he left us we were having coffee together when he leaned across the table and said, "If anything should ever happen to me will you help Mary and the kids tidy up my affairs and keep an eye on them for me?" ... This illustrates the unselfishness of Joe that we all know so well. He was always thinking of others. Who could ever forget his tireless work with the wayward youth of our community?

This last linking sentence invites an example. Richard then relived from memory how Joe had transformed a group of society's troublesome teenagers into a champion chess team who in turn went on to help others.

Richard concluded with: "It's unselfish deeds and qualities like these that will allow us to hold Joe in our hearts forever."

Richard phoned me a week later to say that the inclusion of this information, sensitively presented, made his contribution to the memorial service a moving experience for everyone.

Our formula of 'Past, Present, Future' would work perfectly in a memorial situation. You could reminisce about how things were then, give an example of how much she is missed now, and share your thoughts on how she will be remembered.

> **Tip:** Notice how Richard used phrases such as 'journey to the beyond' and 'before he left us' in place of the abrupt 'died' or 'dead'. We all know they are dead, but these gentle phrases somehow soften the blow and ease the pain ...

It's okay to cry

Some time ago a friend of mine had to speak at a special function in her honour after 30 years of service with the same organisation. "I need some help," she pleaded over the phone. It turned out that her greatest fear was what would happen when she came to the part of mentioning her dear husband who had recently lost a long battle with cancer. Everyone knew how devotedly she had nursed her life-long partner for two years as he lay dying. Everyone knew how much she adored him. And Janine knew how deeply her friends and colleagues cared, even though words don't come easy in such times of trial. "I'll be okay sharing the lighter moments of my experiences at work, but I don't think I could handle talking about Jim." She then fell silent.

"Janine," I said quietly, "let me share an experience I had in one of my public speaking workshops."

The brief was for everyone to relive an experience that had left a lasting impression on them. When Heather got up to speak this is what we heard:

> I was just like any 13-year-old girl experiencing the normal joy and pain of growing up. This particular night I had exchanged especially harsh words with my mother over some trivial observation she had made about the untidiness of my room.
>
> This heated exchange culminated in me storming off to my bedroom screaming, "I really hate you!"

That night while I slept my mother passed away.

Days later, and absolutely grief-stricken, I found a letter addressed to me in the drawer of my mother's dressing room table. It read:

Dearest Heather,

Mummy has been sick for a long time. I've tried to keep it from you in the hope that I'd get better. Please forgive some of the things I've said and done over these past 12 months as I've never meant to hurt you.

I love you very much and will forever,

Your loving mother.

This letter remains one of my most cherished possessions. If only I could turn the clock back I'd make sure the last words I'd shared with my mother were words of love rather than words of hate.

There wasn't a dry eye in the room. Some people were actually sobbing. And I had to stand up and give feedback on the effectiveness of this courageous talk!

Holding back the tears, I walked to the front of the room and opened my mouth to speak, but the lump in my throat prevented anything from coming out. There was nothing I could do but let the tears flow. Slowly, I regained my composure, dried my eyes with a tissue and had a sip from a glass of water. I was now ready to share my thoughts on why Heather's talk was so effective in appealing to both heart and mind.

"The secret is," I told Janine, "under no circumstances apologise for something which is as natural as the air we breathe. Just let the tears flow. And as you do, the audience members' tears will flow with you. Dry your eyes with your handkerchief if it makes you feel better. Have a sip of water. Glance at your notes for your next key idea, and then gently pick up from where you left off. Believe me, you'll soon regain your composure and be able to share some of those lighter moments with your colleagues and friends."

The important thing to remember is that during this time the communication continues. Your listeners have become sharers of a powerful silence that mere words could never express.

Janine later reported that all went exceptionally well. When she broached the subject of her husband she simply let the tears flow without any apology. She gave her audience permission to share in her grief with a story they could all relate to. After one especially traumatic episode where she'd almost given up hope, young Martin at the front desk had reached out and touched her on the shoulder. "We do care," he said simply.

"These three words," Janine told her listeners, "said it all." Now everyone had tears in their eyes.

The interesting thing is that five minutes later Janine had everyone laughing with a lighter story – exactly as we'd planned. At times of intense sadness and grief people appreciate any emotional release. If you share an anecdote reflecting the lighter moments of life, laughter, as well as tears, will help a lot.

I experienced this recently at a moving memorial service for my Auntie Flo. A eulogy by her son choked us up as he shared the incredible sacrifices she had made for her family, yet he also shared some of the fun and drama generated by this remarkable woman with a couple of anecdotes illustrating her no-nonsense approach to life. This release allowed us to laugh long and loud, and we appreciated that.

Everything on this earth is relevant. Auntie Flo's memorial service in that little chapel was just as moving, just as inspiring and timeless as Lord Spencer's beautiful eulogy for Lady Di in Westminster Abbey. By following the simple steps outlined in this book, the words you share with your friends and family at a time of such deep sadness will have the same lasting effect.

Adding humour to your presentation

Another deep-seated anxiety I come across is the fear of an audience expecting you to be funny. For many years Brendon was haunted by this fear. His long-time business partner had an innate knack of being funny – whenever he'd stand up to speak he'd have his audiences in fits of laughter. "I just couldn't compete," Brendon told me. "In the end I'd automatically hand any public speaking over to Jim because he had the natural talent."

For more than a decade Brendon lived in the shadow of his flamboyant colleague. The crazy thing is that he spent most of his time persuasively speaking in a courtroom as one of Melbourne's leading barristers! Brendon had fallen for the old trap of comparing himself to others. So what if his business partner was hilariously funny? Good on him! There will always be people more humorous – and less humorous – than ourselves. We've got to purge ourselves of the inhibiting mindset that some individuals among us have a monopoly on all the humour while the rest of us are left to cheer them on.

Using the approach outlined in this book, Brendon rid himself of this ingrained notion once and for all with a story he told at his son's 21st birthday party. He discovered that humour from our own experiences has our unique stamp on it.

The funny side of life

He began by thanking everybody for being there to celebrate such an important occasion, and stating how proud everyone was of Michael's achievements and his responsible approach to life.

Then he set the scene by describing a characteristic about his son his friends and family could identify with: "One thing I'll say about Michael, he's always been fiercely independent." He then relived from memory how Michael would never let anyone help him cut his food when learning to use a knife and fork as a young child. He had his listeners eavesdropping on a scene at the table so they could witness what was going on for themselves. "No! I do self!" they heard little Michael stubbornly declare; dangerously brandishing his knife and fork. " ... Hasn't changed a great deal," Brendon added dryly. "It's a bit like the time we embarked on our one-and-only driving lesson a couple of years ago."

Brendon then had his audience sitting in the front seat of the car with him as he gave his son those all-important last-minute instructions. "Dad, I've been driving on the farm for two years now," Michael declared indignantly, thrusting the car into reverse and backing out of the driveway at frightening speed. "This is not good," Brendon muttered to himself.

He had his audience visualise his neighbour polishing his brand new BMW on the other side of the road, blissfully unaware that the driver's door of his pride and joy was about to be remodelled. "Everything went into slow motion," he recalled. "All I remember is a dull thud and a sinking feeling as I realised what he'd hit! The whole driving lesson lasted about one minute. Thankfully we were insured."

He rounded the story off with: "I think Michael's fierce independence has mellowed somewhat since then. The other day he said to me, 'Dad? Remember the time *we* hit Bill Snead's car when you were teaching me to drive?'"

He concluded by reiterating just how proud he was of his son's achievements and inviting everyone to join him in drinking a toast to Michael's health and future success. The audience loved it.

For the first time in his life Brendon realised that he could be funny speaking before a group. His listeners had laughed all the way through it. They had reacted to his words just as he had seen them react to the words of the man in whose shadow he had lived for years. He now knows that he has his own way of being funny and he hasn't looked back since.

The important lesson to remember here is, we are not comedians, we are speakers. Comedians are expected to be funny. They study the art of comedy like a science. A speaker on the other hand is not expected to be funny, but when we are it's a bonus!

Involve your audience

If, during proceedings, you notice someone saying something clever or memorable, make a mental note of it, or better still jot it down for possible use as a running joke. Reference to it later in your talk not only generates laughs but also shows you have been listening to your audience. I remember a young newlywed couple who arrived late one night at a function and the chairman announced that they had just returned from their honeymoon. Later, when a speaker was invited to come forward and say a few words, he said that – unlike Mary and John – he had yet to get his act together. Everyone, including Mary and John, enjoyed the comment.

Being thrown by the wits and the wags

When you are speaking, don't be afraid of being thrown or upstaged by the wits and the wags in your audience calling out funny things. Encourage them! Some comments from the audience can be hilariously funny. Join in the fun with little asides and laugh right along with them. They can't take over because you are in control. If some clever quip does distract you, coolly glance at your notes for your next central idea and continue as if this interaction was the most natural thing in the world. Our friend Brendon told me that during the above story about his son's first driving lesson the best laughs came from a couple of his son's friends in the audience calling out funny things, yet it was Brendon who got the accolades for being an entertaining speaker! And this interaction played its part in taking the pressure off him.

Tip: If you want to make a point by poking fun at somebody, poke it at yourself. People like to know you're prone to the same mistakes as everyone else. A story against yourself will help you connect with your listeners and their human frailties.

Even in the direst of circumstances there's a funny side. As a professional conference speaker I take immense pride in whatever I do on the platform. Some time back, and under the critical eye of my peers, I was Master of Ceremonies for the National Speakers Association of Australia's Annual General Meeting in the Grand Ballroom at the Hyatt in Melbourne. It was a most prestigious affair, with row upon row of influential people smiling back at me. After inviting our treasurer to come forward and present her report I politely stepped back – and disappeared off the back of the stage! To make matters worse, on the way down I caught my foot in the hem of the backdrop curtain and brought that down with me. When I stood up, arms flailing all over the place, I looked like an Egyptian mummy trying to break loose from its shroud. By the time I had disentangled myself and crawled back on stage the audience was out of control. People were howling with laughter. I clambered back on stage doing my best to straighten myself out and reintroduced our mildly amused treasurer … this time stepping warily to the side. I was told later that "a treasure's report has never been so much fun!" I've been circumspect of elevated platforms ever since and I have a great story to use when I need it.

Hindsight enables us to share an uncomfortable situation with our listeners and actually enjoy it because this time we're merely observers!

One last word – beware of the use of jokes in your talk. A friend of mine recently opened a business presentation with a joke. The joke fell flat and set the atmosphere for the rest of his talk. Why run the risk? If you are good at telling jokes and have a bag full of funny one-liners to get you out of trouble, great. But if you're like the majority of us, I strongly suggest you don't try to compete with professional comedians. You'll find a wealth of humour in the real-life situations that unfold around you. I recall my little boy once coming into the kitchen wearing a cardboard monkey mask he had just coloured in. He also had his pants around his ankles. "Pull your pants up," I said. "But Daaaad … " he said indignantly, "I'm a baboon and they show their bottoms!"

Of course I've filed that one away for the right audience at the right time. Be on the lookout for these priceless gems. To add humour to your talk, all you have to do is use a story such as this. Pete Crofts, Australia's foremost humour coach, says, "Everybody needs a good laugh, not only to enjoy themselves and be successful, but to help them grow and understand one another." I know of no better way for a speaker to achieve this than share a simple story of life that people can relate to.

Chapter 6 Key points

- Draw on your own experiences or ask friends and relatives for stories you can use.

- Use the 'Past, Present, Future' formula.

- Never compete with alcohol for attention. Arrange to speak around 8 o'clock when the tables are cleared.

- At a memorial service, let the tears flow if that's what comes naturally. Do not apologise. You'll soon regain your composure and be able to continue.

- At times of intense sadness and grief people appreciate any emotional release. Share one or two 'lighter' moments with your listeners and they'll respond with laughter for they'll need it as much as you do.

Monitoring your progress Exercise 7

The following three public speaking scenarios will give you the opportunity of putting into practice the techniques you have learned so far. Analyse each situation to determine what techniques and approaches apply, then briefly answer the questions. Since the wording of your answers will not be exactly the same as the model answers in the Answer Key, on page 199, use your own judgment in marking your responses right or wrong.

1. You are a young woman about to leave your job for wider horizons. A number of your close friends have organised a goodbye party in your honour where you'll be expected to give a speech. You feel fairly comfortable with your immediate work mates in administration, but you're a little uneasy about speaking in front of the folk from the warehouse you don't know that well. Your purpose is to thank everyone for their friendship and personal growth you've experienced with the company and what this means to you. To achieve this you'll have to relate to everyone and connect with all of them on a personal level. The challenge for you is to bridge this slight 'them and us' gap.

   a. What aspects of teamwork could you reflect on to bring the warehouse folk into the picture and make them feel important?

   b. What social occasions could provide an 'inside' story that will help you bond both parties together in a light-hearted manner?

   c. Keeping in mind who these people are, describe your overall approach to the situation as you prepare your talk.

2. You are a young man in your early twenties. You've recently learned that your best friend has been tragically killed in a car accident. Prior to his burial, his distraught parents ask that as a close friend would you mind sharing some special thoughts

at the memorial service. Saddened beyond belief, yet touched by this request, a picture begins to emerge of the wonderful times you had together and the strength of your friendship. You decide to take your fellow mourners on a brief journey from the first time you met Damien to the night you read about the tragic news of his death on social media. Your purpose is to highlight his musical genius and his readiness to always share with others. You take care to reduce tension with a humorous anecdote along the way and finish with a story of inspiration and hope. Visualise yourself delivering this talk for a few minutes each day. You actually experience the sadness, the laughter and the tears. You do not see yourself apologising for your feelings. You see yourself celebrating the life of an unforgettable person.

o   What is the purpose of the above talk?

o   Keeping in mind the sombre mood of this audience, briefly describe three techniques, strategies, or approaches you discern in the above scenario.

3.   You are a middle-aged scientist and widely respected for your study of amphibians. You have been invited to address a non-academic function as an after-dinner speaker. Aware that people appreciate something light and entertaining after a sumptuous meal and a glass of wine, your catchy topic sets the tone of your talk: 'Australia, Frogs, and the Promise of Things to Come!' In the 25 minutes you have to share with your audience, you decide on three amusing incidents you've experienced with frogs in Australia that will promote your central theme: frogs are our environmental barometers. You'll relive these incidents from memory. And you'll also encourage the occasional wisecrack from the audience aware that this interaction generates laughs, breaks down barriers, and takes the pressure off you. Each amusing story will promote a few chuckles, create a bit of drama, and lead to a point. Each story suggests the next as you build to your conclusion: "The humble frog indeed promises much if we all play our part in looking after the world we live in ... for if frogs go, we're in trouble!"

o   More accustomed to lecturing to conservative colleagues in academic circles, you tailor this talk to a general audience and a specific after-dinner occasion. What is the difference between the two approaches?

o   Using your imagination, describe three reasons why you'd enjoy this talk if you were part of this audience.

CHAPTER 7

Thinking on your feet under pressure

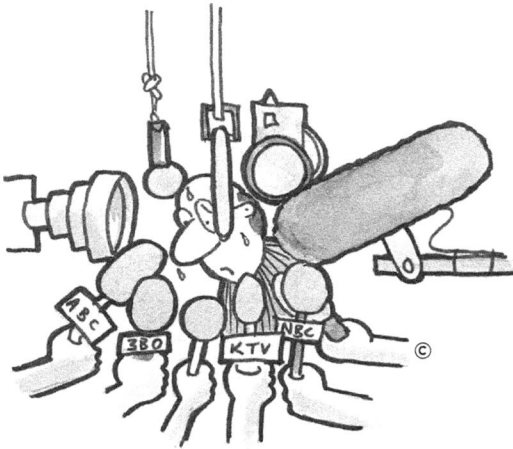

A common fear among people I talk to is the fear of being asked to stand up and speak without any preparation. This could be the proverbial 'few words' at a social occasion, a contribution at a meeting, or being spokesperson in a time of crisis. You could be put on the spot to thank someone, introduce a speaker or field questions from the floor. In all these cases panic can rear its ugly head and totally destroy your composure. By the end of this chapter you'll have the know-how and self-confidence to be in control and acquit yourself well when this happens to you.

Preparing for the unexpected

Here's a way to get rid of 95 per cent of the fear of impromptu speaking in one go. It's what I call 'prepared spontaneity'! "Making the unexpected the expected!" In my programs I say to people, "If you have the remotest inkling that you might be called on to speak, what would be the logical, sensible thing to do?"

They think a little, then tentatively say, "Prepare something?"

And they're dead right!

But what do you prepare? Before the event, seek out some knowledge of the meeting you will be attending and the people who will be there. In an impromptu situation they really don't expect a polished, planned talk. But we can at least anticipate this eventuality by preparing something to say beforehand. Our little 'Loop Method' formula of 'tell 'em what you're going to say, tell 'em, then tell 'em again' would be perfect! So think of a point you'd like to make to this particular group and a story you could use to illustrate this point in action. You won't think very clearly on your feet unless you've done some clear thinking before you get on your feet! That master of language Mark Twain once said, "It takes me about three weeks to prepare a good impromptu speech."

And don't forget to write out a purpose sentence embodying the point you wish to make as you plan and rehearse your talk. Back it up with an example that connects with the hearts and minds of your listeners. Breathe life into your story by reliving something that happened to you, something you read or saw on television, or a case study you are familiar with. Conclude by restating your main point again. Quietly reflect on this for a short while, not to remember it word for word, but to be at home with the example you wish to share and the point you want it to illustrate. Now you are ready for them. With this package of 'prepared spontaneity' in your pocket, the unexpected will become the expected and no longer frighten you. But how many people actually do this?

If you're not prepared for the 'unexpected' and you've just arrived on the scene to learn the guest speaker can't make it and you're the bunny in the firing line, the same system applies. Only this time you have a matter of minutes to get your thoughts together. Find yourself a quiet corner and write down your purpose sentence, which is the thought you'll echo for your conclusion. Now latch on to an experience the audience can relate to that illustrates the purpose you just wrote down. The first thing that comes to mind is all you are after. It's now a matter of stating your case, reliving your example and then restating your main point. That's it. That's all you have to do. And don't worry about not saying enough for there is a wise adage in speaking: tell them what you have to say then sit down!

If, on the other hand, it really is a case of being thrown to the wolves, where the first you hear of your contribution is when you're announced, our tried-and-proven formula of 'Past, Present, Future' will come to the rescue!

Past, present, future saves the day

I once found myself stepping onto the platform in front of 200 wildly cheering Italians as the recipient of the 'Best Actor' award for my role as Pontius Pilate in The Easter Passion Play. So much was I taken by surprise that I hadn't a clue what I was going to say. I'd broken my own cardinal rule of not preparing something beforehand when there was even the slightest chance I could be called on to speak. Then, like a godsend, I remembered …

Past: All I had to do here was relive something relevant from the past:

> At the audition Michael handed me a script and said "Read this". "But", I protested, "This is Pontius Pilate … a lead role!" "You'll be okay," Michael persisted. "Just read it for me." After a few lines he said, "You'll do. You're our Pontius Pilate … But don't worry we'll help you." And help me you people did … For six months you helped me with my Italian pronunciation and interpretation of the character. But most of all you helped me to understand myself.

Sharing the spotlight with those who help us adds a human touch to the acceptance. Few people ever achieve anything entirely alone.

Present: Then on to the second step of commenting on the here and now (which you don't really have to think about – the present just 'appears'):

> And to stand here today with this plaque is truly one of the most memorable events of my life … for this award is as much yours as it is mine. It will hang on my wall and I'll look at it with pride.

People love to know what you're going to do with a gift.

Future: All I had to do here was speculate …

> I'm sure the confidence I've gained from the experience will stay with me forever. And if you need a Pontius Pilate for next year's production just give me a call. I'd love to be part of it.

To a person they cheered, because unknown to them, I had a simple formula that enabled me to confidently convey my heartfelt thanks.

> **Tip:** When presenting an award or gift, hold the item in your left hand so that your right hand is free to shake the recipient's hand. If you're the receiver of the award or gift and it is wrapped, say, "Do you mind if I open it?" Grown-ups never lose the childlike excitement of a present being opened.

Keep your eyes and ears open

Have a pen and pad handy and keep your eyes and ears open on the night for items of interest you can refer to – this will personalise your talk; take your cues from the previous speaker or describe the scene in front of you; talk about your listeners, who they are and what they do; talk about the occasion and the circumstances that brought you to the meeting.

Handling the media in a time of crisis

In a time of crisis, stay cool and don't let anyone rattle you, even if it seems as if the world is falling down around your ears. The Chief Traffic Officer of a regional city council had to face a hostile media after the controversial introduction of parking meters to the city centre. "They absolutely crucified me," he told me later. "I was made to look an incompetent fool."

After some discussion Bill realised that journalists and radio announcers are always after a good story, and if they smell blood all the better! They want a lively, interesting interview. They were not attacking him personally, he just happened to be the person in the hot seat. He also realises he could have taken control of the interview with a little forethought about what points he could have made to give his position a positive spin. He could also have brought some breathing space by saying, "I can't talk right now, could you ring me back in 15 minutes."

If you're in the hot seat like Bill, accept the possibility that a curly question will most probably come your way. So waste no time in brainstorming all the emotionally charged questions they could throw at you: "What went wrong?", "Were you aware of the slush fund?", or, "How would you react if this toxic dump was near your children?" Then, no matter what they ask, you'll be able to refer back to the points you want to make. Now you're ready to play your game, not theirs.

Politicians are good at this. They often don't answer the question put to them. Many steer the discussion where they want it to go with stock phrases such as, "The reality is ... ", or, "The fact of the matter is ... " Former Australian Prime Minister Malcolm Fraser says sticky questions never fazed him. He'd simply say, "The real question you should be asking is … "and then proceed to answer the question he posed himself! Show genuine concern if appropriate, but the secret is to steer the conversation back to the positive things you're doing about the situation.

Tip: Keep repeating your central points over and over – this makes it hard to edit them out. It also helps people who have just tuned in to catch your main point.

Introducing a speaker

The purpose of an introduction is to capture attention, excite your audience, and have the speaker step into an atmosphere of warmth and expectation. I once saw an administration official introduce a hapless City Councillor to a group of hopping-mad ratepayers as 'one of the heavies from Head Office'. You can imagine the warm reception she received!

Tip: People are not being rude when you find them talking as you step forward to introduce someone. When there's nothing happening it's natural for people talk to each other. The fact that they are there is a tremendous compliment in itself! Radiate warmth and friendliness, and say: "Thank you ladies and gentlemen, could I have your attention please … " and wait … and wait. Look for a friendly face and say it again: "Your attention please … " and wait some more! Calmness will settle over the audience until there's absolute silence. Only then do you begin to speak. This all comes across as natural and normal.

Take control of the situation and contact the speaker beforehand for their bio and relevant information, then craft their introduction along the lines of the following explanation.

I was once Master of Ceremonies for the Fleet Association of Australia's annual conference. The night before, I'd spent a good deal of time tailoring introductions for each guest speaker to ensure the audience would be eager to hear who they were and what they had to say. All I had to do now was read these introductions out. But even the best laid plans can come undone. On the day only three of the listed speakers turned up, and I met their replacements 10 minutes before they were due to speak!

"I'm speaking in place of Sue Smith," one person nonchalantly announced, handing me a sheaf of information to 'help' me with the introduction. There was a time when this would have sent me into a complete tailspin. Luckily I have another formula at my disposal which allows me to formulate an introduction for any person, on any subject in just a few minutes. It's what I call the 'SRQ' formula: 'Subject', 'Relevance', 'Qualify.'

I quickly took each speaker aside and wrote down the subject and title of their talk for step one (if they didn't have one, we quickly decided on one). I then went on to gain a quick overview of the content and purpose of their talk. As we spoke, I jotted down a central idea of why each topic was relevant to this audience for step two. For step three some pertinent questions furnished me with one or two 'achievements' to qualify each speaker's right to speak. A quick revision of my notes helped me clarify the logic of these three steps. Fortified with these precious 'SRQ' jottings, I confidently strode to the lectern, stated a title and subject, explained why it was relevant to this audience and why the speaker was 'qualified' to speak on the subject. That day my introductions were interesting and effective, all because this simple formula came to my rescue. Let me give you a detailed example of how this simple formula can work with any topic and any person – no matter who they are!

Let's imagine that your guest speaker is a leading cardiac specialist and you have the task of introducing her to the audience. Her topic is, 'The Heart of the Matter.' Your time to make yourself known to the speaker and take some hurried notes is limited.

Step one: 'Subject': Acknowledge guests of honour and welcome everyone, then state the title of the presentation, create a context and establish the importance of the topic.

> Distinguished guests, ladies and gentlemen, it's now time to introduce our guest speaker. Her subject is 'The Heart of the Matter'. Today, people live longer and are more conscious about their health, yet heart disease remains one of our biggest killers!"

That's it. That's all you have to do for step one.

Step two: 'Relevance': Tell your listeners how this topic is relevant to them. Set up an air of 'agreement' by finding common ground with your audience.

> I guess it would be safe to say that everyone here tonight has been touched in some way by a friend or loved one as a result of heart disease. The good news is that, unlike a few short years ago, you and I can do a lot to ensure we don't cut our lives short through ignorance. Our speaker tonight will show us how.

Step three: 'Qualify': For this last step, state the 'qualifications' of the speaker. This will have your audience thinking, "We are in the presence of an expert, someone who has earned the right to be here."

> For more than 30 years our eminent guest has studied the heart and all its functions in many of the world's leading institutions. She is the author of six books and has published more than 200 papers on the subject. And more recently she has pioneered an electronic device that promises to revolutionise

our entire approach to heart surgery. To share a little of her passion with us tonight ... would you please welcome Dr Jane Hartman.

You now lead the applause until the speaker takes her place on the platform, then move to the side.

In most cases you won't be introducing a world-renowned heart specialist. It's more likely to be a young person who has done something outstanding, or a local identity whose claim to fame is their achievements and unique experience. In this case, for step three, outline two or three of these achievements and experiences to qualify the speaker. They are just as valid as impressive academic qualifications.

Of course, the ideal situation would be that you have ample time to reflect on the speaker's background and achievements using this formula as a framework for their introduction and prepare it beforehand, but we don't always have this luxury! And always read your written introductions, especially if you have a series of speakers to introduce. An introduction is the one occasion where it's preferable to read your words formulated from the information given to you.

Now all you need do when asked to introduce a speaker with little or no notice is use the 'SRQ' formula.

Let's summarise those three simple steps again.

Immediately take control and seek out the speaker you'll be introducing. As you chat, jot down the title and context for step one. For step two, begin to formulate an emotional hook, a universal statement that will set up an air of agreement in the audience, arouse their expectations, and warm them towards the speaker. And finally, for step three, glean two or three 'achievements' to qualify the speaker. Then consolidate these three sequential thoughts for a minute or two. The system never fails. Use it and it won't fail you either.

Tip: Always be positive about a speaker and make sure you pronounce their name clearly and correctly.

You as the guest speaker

If *you* are the guest speaker, make it easy for the person introducing you by writing your own introduction. No-one knows you better than you do. And don't be faint hearted when praising yourself, for it is someone else who will be saying these wonderful things about you. A great introduction will make the person introducing you look good too, and they'll appreciate that! The following is an example of one of mine.

Introduction for Laurie Smale
(Kindly read as if you compiled this intro yourself.)

Now it's time to introduce our guest speaker ... author of the best-selling book **How to Take The Panic Out of Public Speaking**. He has helped thousands cast off their fears and speak with confidence ... be it with one person or in front of hundreds!

He has written five books on communicating confidence that sell in their thousands. He is a Master Speaking Coach, and is in great demand as an inspirational speaker.

But nothing came easy for him ... In his early years he suffered the pain, the fear, and the humiliation of many a public speaking disaster himself ... until he figured out how the 'gifted few' make it look so easy!

To let us in on the secret too ... please welcome Laurie Smale!

Can you see how a carefully crafted introduction like this will set you up for a win? I always go out of my way to ensure the person introducing me gets a copy of my intro a few days before my talk. I strongly advise you do the same. But I always bring an extra copy with me on the day!

> **TIP:** Note the specific direction at the top of my prepared introduction: kindly read this introduction as if you compiled it yourself. This is because a person once introduced me with the words: "I'll now read this piece of paper that Laurie gave me," severely denting my credibility! This clear directive not only avoids this happening; it makes the person introducing you look and feel good; and ensures you have a fine reputation to live up to.

Of course, the above example is the ideal scenario, but sometimes there'll be no-one to introduce you so you'll have to establish your credibility by citing your credentials in a low-key manner yourself. Here's how I would tactfully weave the same things into my opening remarks so it doesn't sound like I'm bragging and put people off:

> As someone who speaks and coaches for a living, it's interesting how I've grown from a person with very little confidence into someone who can now comfortably express myself before groups ... This evening I'd like to share some of my hard-earned secrets with you so you can walk out of this room with a new understanding of it all and start treading this exciting path yourself ... How does that sound?

I have aroused the curiosity of my listeners, and they will be thinking, "This person has earned the right to speak on this subject ... Tell me more!"

Thanking a speaker

Another talk that can be sprung on you by surprise is being asked to thank a speaker. What do you say? How do you prevent yourself from rambling on? This time we have a little two-step formula to make thanking a speaker a cinch. For step one, use the person's first name for warmth and simply replay an example from the talk to show you were listening:

> Thank you Mary ... Your way with words is amazing ... We will never forget that frightened little girl being ridiculed in front of the whole class. This unforgettable image will serve as a constant reminder of how not to treat people ... and we thank you for that.

Note how I use the more inclusive pronoun 'we' rather than 'I'. Remember you are not expressing your personal thanks, you are thanking the speaker on behalf of the audience.

For step two, invite everyone to join you in thanking the guest speaker. Remember that people are waiting for you to lead the applause. This time use the speaker's full name and title:

> Would you please join me in thanking our very special guest speaker tonight, the President of our organisation, Mary Thomas.

An ideal 'thank you' should last no longer than one minute. The essence of your heartfelt thanks, however, could stay with the speaker for years.

> **Tip:** You might thank the speaker by way of a personal incident from your own life that relates to their talk. The secret here is to cut out all the detail and shorten it down to a couple of sentences. In a talk titled 'Cooking up a Storm', I immediately identified with the plight of the speaker. In my thank you I said: "I know how you must have felt when your guests arrived ... reminds me of my first attempt at cooking where some exotic egg dish I'd attempted ended up all over the stove and the floor ... " Both audience and speaker enjoyed this and could see I'd been listening with genuine interest to the talk.

Keep it positive

"If you can't say anything nice, don't say anything at all," admonished Thumper The Rabbit's mother in the Disney classic *Bambi*. This saying has now entered into folklore and is one we should pay heed to. No matter how uninspiring or boring a presentation is, it's not our job to have a dig at the speaker. The very nature of thanking someone is positive, so always look for the good – that's our task. You won't gain any respect by having a cheap shot at a speaker who has just bombed out.

I once had to thank a statistical expert from the Bureau of Statistics at a national education conference in Canberra. For 40 minutes she rattled off sterile educational facts and figures from a sheaf of papers without looking up once! The sustained applause at the end was due to sheer relief that the ordeal was finally over. Many people were fighting to stay awake. And I had to get up and say something positive!

Here's what I said:

> Thank you Jennifer for that very informative presentation. You certainly have a passion for numbers! We do appreciate the time and effort you've obviously put into collating the latest statistical information in a way that makes sense to us. I'm sure that from this vast array of facts and figures there was something in there for everybody!

I then went on to invite everyone to join me in thanking Jennifer for her valuable contribution to the conference. Later a person came up to me and wryly said, "You handled that well." And you can too, even if the only positive thing you can find to comment on is the speaker's courage.

Tip: Don't rob people of the joy of giving. If someone goes out of their way to say thank you, don't make them feel bad by saying things like: "It was awful, I left half of it out!" Instead, learn to accept words of thanks in the spirit in which they're given. Say, "Thank you, I'm glad you got something out of it." Remember, you are the only one who knows what you left in or out of your talk!

Questions from the floor

During question time, many people are self-conscious of being evaluated or saying something that might highlight their ignorance. Consequently, many stimulating ideas remain unsaid. Renowned speaker Glen Capelli says he never launches into question time with the somewhat brusque, "Are there any questions?" He prefers a more gentle approach where he invites people to turn and ask each other what it all means to them. When everyone is 'primed' with concrete things to say, he asks, "Has anyone got any further observations, comments or questions?"

Another friendly approach to break down communicating inhibitions in the audience could be to ask the first question yourself: "When sharing these ideas, a question I'm often asked is … [here state the question]" Preface your answer with, "And what I say is … " Then ask your audience, "Who has the next question?", as if a listener had proffered the first one! You could also seed the audience with a couple of your friends to ask questions to start the ball rolling. Once somebody breaks the ice others have the confidence to share their thoughts and feelings on the subject too.

Remember not to direct your answer only to the person who asks the question. Thank the person for asking the question then direct your response to the whole audience. This way you will include everybody in the interaction, whether they ask a question or not.

Respond with a story

Once during question time the erudite Australian historian Professor Blainey was asked if he had any idea of what it must have felt like to be a rural settler in early Australia. He let his mind tick over for a few seconds then answered the question with a story. He told of the time he and his mate got a job stacking hay in Victoria's harsh wheat-growing Mallee region during the holidays when they were about 15. I'll never forget the image of those two young boys sweating it out in the blazing sun, pitching hay high up on to a horse-drawn cart while the farmer straddled the top of the heap lording it over them. This simple incident more than answered the question of what early settler life might have been like.

> **Tip:** On occasion you could invite questions during your presentation rather than having an allotted question time at the end. This injects a dynamic two-way feel into your talk, and helps you stay in control and finish with impact. Not only that, it takes the pressure of you!

Be honest

If you don't know the answer to a particular question, simply say so. People are reasonable. They understand that you can't know everything there is to know and that information changes quickly nowadays. Usually a friendly, "See me over coffee and I'll point you in the right direction," will suffice. If you don't know an answer that you should know, be honest and own up to the fact. I was once at a parent information night at our local school. During question time the sports coordinator was asked about the printed programs that were supposed to be there for the Twilight Carnival that was in two days. She said, "To be honest they're sitting at home on my desk. I was up till 1 am marking papers and I simply rushed out this morning and forgot them ... and I apologise for this. They'll be available at the front desk from 8:30 am tomorrow."

I remember thinking to myself, *That's fair enough. I've been guilty of the same sort of thing myself* ... and not giving it another thought. I sensed that most other parents felt this way too. By being honest and admitting up front what had happened we accepted that she was subject to the same human frailties as the rest of us!

Sticky questions

On rare occasions a person will persist with something controversial or outside the scope of your talk. Under no circumstances should you become involved in a one-on-one exchange. I learned long ago that it's never wise to argue with a fool because bystanders don't know which is which. If your friendly offer to talk to them later doesn't work, simply cease to look at them and move on to your next point. Most times, however, you'll be on firm ground and be able to draw on your experience for an adequate answer.

An effective communicator never ever uses sarcasm. You'll run the risk of getting everyone offside. Instead, try to make the person giving you a hard time feel that their contribution is important: "Thank you for the question ... that's a valid point. We cover that later on." It's important you keep your promise and do so, otherwise you'll lose credibility. People are entitled to their opinion. Don't agree or disagree with the questioner's point, just state that it is valid.

Your audience as a resource

Never be intimidated by those in the audience who know more about your subject than you do. Draw on them as a resource. Your listeners will sense your ability to interact with people as a natural part of your presentation. Once during a business presentation a young woman asked me, "How do I cope with being asked to facilitate a meeting between six senior engineers on a subject I have very little knowledge of?" As I stood there formulating an answer, a man raised his hand and said, "I can answer that." I gratefully nodded in his direction.

He went on to say that recently he had found himself in a similar situation with some senior scientific people. He realised that his job was not to pit himself against their overwhelming knowledge; his task was to make people feel welcome, stimulate discussion, and steer the meeting to its expected outcome as per the agenda.

I watched the young woman listen carefully as this man spoke. When he had finished I said to the woman, "Does that answer your question?"

"Oh yes, thank you," she replied. So when someone offers a contribution in response to a question from the audience, welcome it. You will all be the richer for it.

Throw the question back to the audience

At other times you could be proactive in answering a tricky question by throwing it back to the audience. At a presentation on 'How to Pool Your Talents and Work as a Team' for the Junior Chamber of Commerce, I was momentarily stumped for an answer when a member of the audience asked: "Do you return to a hierarchical structure if a program on self-empowerment is not working?" Momentarily thrown, I transferred this complex question to my listeners by inviting them to reflect on what they thought about it. Instantly all the pressure was off me and on to them! The spontaneous open forum that followed enabled me to contribute something intelligent on the subject by bouncing off their ideas, and the audience felt that they had played an integral part in contributing to the response.

Repeat the question

Always repeat the question for the benefit of those who may not have heard it clearly. People find it quite annoying for a speaker to listen to a question from someone in the front row and then proceed to answer in great detail a question that most of the audience didn't hear! If the question is complex or convoluted, reword it and play it back to confirm that you have the question right. And after your response, go back to the person and check that they are satisfied with the answer.

Tip: If a question is particularly sticky, buy a little time to formulate an answer by having a sip from your glass of water.

Trusting your own knowledge

Here's a great idea to help enrich your answers during question time. Dr Michael Hewitt-Gleeson, author of *Software for the Brain*, tells of an experience he had with Edward De Bono, the legendary pioneer of lateral thinking, during a meeting with some very influential people. Hewitt-Gleeson noticed that whatever question was put to his esteemed colleague, he always found something relevant and worthwhile to say.

Afterwards he said to De Bono, "I've twigged to what you are doing ... No matter what question you are asked, you say something like: 'There are two points to make here ...' knowing full well that something relevant will flow from your subconscious bank of ideas." And if you think about it, isn't this the way everyday conversation works? We are continually using ideas, impressions and experiences that are stored in our minds and they seem to come to the forefront all by themselves. Have you ever been walking down the street and heard a familiar sound or smelled some freshly-baked bread and an image comes to your mind that you haven't thought of for years? We are talking about the same thing here, only we are in control of the retrieval system. Here's the sentence I use in my version of De Bono's marvellous little technique: "The interesting thing about this is ... " The secret is to completely trust in your mind to bring forth a relevant piece of information from its vast retrieval system — and that's exactly what will happen.

Let's try a small experiment here to prove my point. Think of a current issue in the news or at home – anything from the Covid 19 pandemic to buying birdseed for your canary. Now with this issue in mind – and without any forethought – say out loud, "The interesting thing about this is … " You'll be amazed at just how easy it is to say something relevant about it.

Practise using this phrase, or versions of it, as a part of your everyday conversation, and try it with different issues.

Close question time with impact

Here's how to ensure your listeners walk away remembering your main message and not the answer to your last question. Take control of the end of the session with an observation such as, "Time has caught up with us … we have time for one more question … "When you have answered this question, restate the main message of your talk once again. That is, repeat your conclusion. How many speakers do you hear waste this opportunity by completing their talk with some wishy washy comment like, "That's about it … " The secret is, immediately after your last answer jump in with, "So remember … ", and confidently replay your conclusion again … the very reason you're giving the talk! Now the Chairperson knows you've finished and will begin their 'thank you'.

Chapter 7 Key points

- No matter what you are asked, don't take things personally. Reporters are always after a good story – the more controversial the better.

- The very nature of thanking someone is a positive exercise so always look for something good to say.

- Don't direct your answer exclusively to the person who asked the question. First repeat the question for those who didn't hear it clearly, then include the rest of the audience in your response.

- Never be intimidated by those in the audience who know more about a subject than you do. Use them as a resource by warmly inviting them to enhance your talk.

Monitoring your progress Exercise 8

Fill in the blanks

Fill in the blanks of the following sentences to see what strategies you'd employ when forced to think on your feet under pressure. Then check your responses in the Answer Key, page 201. Consider your answers correct if they mean the same thing.

(a) If you have the remotest inkling that you might be called on to speak, _____ beforehand.

(b) Be perceived as an off-the-cuff natural in impromptu situations by falling back on the _____, _____, _____, formula.

(c) No matter what questions you are asked in a time of crisis, you will no longer take things _____.

(d) Media people are always after a _____ story, so they'll keep testing you. So stick to the _____ things you are doing about the situation.

(e) An effective introduction should _____ attention and arouse _____.

(f) When thanking a speaker, don't express your personal thanks, you are thanking the speaker on behalf of the _____.

(g) If you don't know the answer to a question, be _____ and simply say so.

(h) The next time a person asks you a question calculated to draw you into a one-on-one exchange, you're going to be polite, keep your _____ and not get sucked into an _____.

(i) Don't leave your audience with the answer to the last question. Seize the opportunity to restate your _____ to reinforce your main message.

CHAPTER 8

Participating in meetings and discussion groups

The general purpose of any meeting is to promote cooperation among the group, exchange ideas, and get something done. An attitude, therefore, of being friendly, courteous, tactful, and open-minded is all important.

And just as important is your new sense of self-worth discovered in these pages. Now you'll be able to lead, and participate in meetings with the knowledge that your ideas and opinions are worth listening to. You didn't just 'fluke' your experiences. You now know you have earned the right to have something to say.

The following insights will ensure that your contribution to meetings and discussion groups will promote cooperation in reaching consensus and getting things done.

Leading a meeting

Chairing a meeting can be very daunting for the fearful and inexperienced speaker. So it was with Jim, a major construction project manager who was secretly terrified of his obligatory weekly progress meetings with the wider corporate world.

The funny thing was he had no problem at all leading his weekly on-the-job updates with his workforce of tradesmen and subcontractors, for in his mind, these weren't 'formal' meetings as such, they were informal gatherings with people he felt comfortable with where a list of workplace problems would be discussed with the aim of solving them.

But it was the offsite formal meetings with all the other corporate stakeholders in their intimidating suits that so daunted him. He told me he'd lie awake at night worrying himself sick about the whole thing, to the point of tossing in his job and doing something else where public speaking wasn't involved! His immediate panic was that his next meeting ordeal was the following week!

My task was to get Jim to walk into this meeting as the 'Project Manager-in-Charge', just as he had been doing every week with his onsite meetings for years. And just as he had been doing successfully in these non-threatening situations, he would be working to an agenda with specific items to discuss and problems to deal with. Only this time his purpose would be to give these people a progress update and answer any concerns they may have … all from the stance of someone who knows a lot more than they do about the intricacies and challenges of the project. Three weeks later I received the following email. (As you read, keep in mind that the big difference with Jim now is he went to that meeting as the proud Project Manager he had earned the right to be – and always had been onsite.

With this positive frame of mind he would be in total control of this project too, even if things didn't run exactly as planned!)

Laurie,

I creamed it man, the meeting went fantastically well!

I woke up at 3 am, my heart was pounding and my chest was tight. The meeting topics were running like mad around my head. I couldn't sleep. I got up and showered, went to work, then realised I had lost my work keys, couldn't get into the office to print out the notes, programs, registers ... not a good start!

Anyway I composed myself, somebody arrived and opened the door and I calmly went about preparing the documents for the 11 am meeting. I started feeling good about myself. I told myself I was in control and it was just a piddly little meeting.

I arrived at the meeting room early and had a little chit chat and coffee with a few people.

I told him to do this to radiate leadership and show he was in control, instead of slinking in at the last minute as he'd always done.

Instead of pushing a bundle of meeting notes down the middle of the table I calmly walked around and handed a copy to each person and said their name as I did it.

I had already met the new guy Gil yesterday. His boss sorta beat me to introducing him, but I sorta busted in and said, "Yes, Gil is new to the project team so why don't we all introduce ourselves and explain what our roles are ... off you go there Sandie." PERFECT! Certainly took the pressure off me!!

I had completely reorganised the notes yesterday to simplify it a tad, it had become somewhat messy to be honest. I then got straight into it and explained the potential issues with the material procurement from overseas and asked everybody for comment/opinion. This really got things buzzing.

For the first time I felt like I was actually chairing a meeting and I was in total control from start to finish … loved it! Only a first step I know, but I feel I'm okay now and can do it.

Thanks for your help Laurie.

Kind regards,

Jim

All Jim really needed was a little help to believe in himself and see things differently.

Keep the following in mind when chairing your meetings:

- *Start the meeting on time:* Starting on time is a courtesy to those who are punctual and encourages latecomers to arrive on time next meeting.

- *Agree on what should be accomplished at the meeting:* After a warm welcome, begin the meeting by discussing and reaching agreement on the purpose and specific objectives of the meeting as per the agenda. With the meeting's objectives clarified up front, members will spend less time discussing irrelevant problems and issues.

Tip: Make sure your introduction provokes immediate discussion without members having to ask for further information on the topic. Start discussion by throwing a question to the group, then keep out of the discussion as far as possible.

- *Allow participants to air conflicting perspectives:* This way the group can address issues constructively. Doing so helps you deal with the possibility of 'hidden agendas', which can sabotage the effectiveness of the meeting if they remain unspoken.

- *Refer to the agenda to keep the meeting on course:* An agenda that has been carefully planned serves as a roadmap for staying on track. (See that each person gets a copy before the meeting.) Encourage the group to identify the costs and benefits of the specified alternative solutions. Discourage discussion of unrelated issues and suggestions which could be dealt with better in another forum.

- *Reaching consensus:* If a consensus cannot be reached on certain issues, confirm what has been agreed upon so far and schedule another meeting – scheduling another meeting is almost always preferable to running a meeting too long and forcing a decision.

Tip: Use a response chart – a sheet with the names of all meeting participants on it – to ensure every member takes some part in the meeting. Each time someone speaks, place a mark opposite the person's name. By tactfully restraining the talkative participants and encouraging the less vocal ones, a better balance is achieved.

Participating in meetings

Be prepared. Get a copy of the meeting agenda beforehand and study it carefully. Look at who is doing what, and where you fit in. Give some thought to your contribution and what you'll say in relation to your specific task and the overall purpose of the meeting. Spend about five minutes a day in quiet reverie with these thoughts in mind. Now, when the meeting comes around you'll participate with confidence because you'll be well prepared.

Just remember that you don't have to have an opinion on everything to be seen as a valuable contributor. One pertinent comment or one strategically placed question is often enough to be seen to move the discussion along and get things done!

> **Tip:** Don't pigeonhole people into little boxes – guard against quick judgment of other members. First impressions are not always valid.

Keep the following in mind when participating in meetings:

- *Start from where they are:* Start from where other members of the meeting are coming from not from where you're at. You have to listen carefully to lead them to where you stand, and then link your ideas to their concerns and hopes. What policy is bothering them? What are they afraid of that might happen tomorrow? What frustrates them today?

- *Use neutral language:* When you have something to say, speak up clearly and distinctly so that all present can hear you. Be sure to use language that is specific and neutral. Emotionally charged terms like "dole bludgers" (a colourful Australian term describing those on government handouts), "let's get real here", or, "what a load of rubbish," generate bad feelings and an unwillingness to cooperate.

> **Tip:** Guard against trying to impose a detailed account of your experiences on the meeting.

- *Get to the nub of the matter:* Make your comments brief. Don't complicate the discussion by airing a view on everything that's been said so far. Stick to the point under discussion and elaborate or answer questions only if prompted to do so.

- *Maintain goodwill:* Never be personal in answering a point. Avoid insulting those you don't happen to agree with. Always direct your comments to the argument, not the person. You can disagree without being disagreeable. Maintain a friendly atmosphere by focusing on ideas and outcomes rather than personalities.

- *Don't monopolise the discussion:* Give others a chance to be heard. Don't get involved in a personal conversation with another member of the group. Other members of the meeting could feel shut out: with valuable contributions left unsaid.

> **Tip:** People can grow and change. A sensitive group can be an agent for that change.

- *Don't be a side talker:* At a meeting a guy once whispered something in my ear about a movie he'd seen the night before. Momentarily distracted, I missed some key information I was keen to hear – and it annoyed me! Don't distract other people with irrelevancies while key points are being discussed by the meeting.

- *Follow-up action:* If you're presenting an idea, be clear with your intentions. Summarise your idea, the pros and cons mentioned, any decision made, and suggest the next follow-up step. Make sure members entrusted with specific actions have a copy of the Meeting Action Statement, page 195 , as a reminder of their obligation.

Create yourself a copy of the Meeting Checklist on the following page to ensure you are well-prepared for a successful meeting.

So now you have it. Enjoy your meetings!

> **Tip:** Abnormal behaviour is a symptom, which has a cause. We need to spend time with people – know and understand them and listen without judgment.

Meeting checklist

The following checklist will help you prepare for, and evaluate, the success of your meeting. Keep it handy for easy reference.

- ☐ Establish a clear objective for the meeting.
- ☐ Research the topic so that you are well informed to lead, or participate, in the meeting.
- ☐ Check the qualifications of other members of the group – their background, experience, status, and ability to contribute in the discussion.
- ☐ Ensure members are given a Meeting Agenda and sufficient information prior to the meeting to enable active participation.
- ☐ Prepare your introduction (or the topic you wish to discuss) making it concise, informative, and challenging.
- ☐ Make an outline of how you propose to lead the session or take part in the meeting.
- ☐ Prepare pertinent questions to ask members if discussion lags, moves too quickly or your point is overlooked.
- ☐ Check that all conference aids are appropriate for the discussion and in good working order.
- ☐ Ensure the room is well lit and ventilated with satisfactory chair arrangements.

CHAPTER 9

Leave nothing to chance

You need to be aware of the problems that can occur when you are giving your talk so you can do your best to avoid them. And most problems, with a bit of planning, can be avoided. In this chapter you will also learn how to rehearse and time your talk.

Venue layout

Just because the room is set up when you arrive at the venue doesn't mean this is the perfect layout for a speaker and audience. Remember that it's *your* talk and you are the one who will look bad if things don't work out because of poor room layout. Always arrive early to befriend staff in case some 'fine tuning' of room layout is needed.

People always respond favourably to a reasonable request if they understand that a slight change is in everyone's interest. On a social occasion such as a wedding reception you often have to run with what is set up. At other times, however, you can have an influence on room layout.

I remember arriving at the Regent in Melbourne for an early morning breakfast talk eager and ready to go, when I walked into a potential disaster. The microphone was set up at the far end of a long, narrow room, making it difficult for the speaker to reach the people at the tables way down the back. Luckily I'd got in early and made friends with the manager and staff. They appreciated the fact that I hadn't lobbed in five minutes before my presentation demanding all their handiwork be rearranged. As a result we were able to relocate the microphone and lectern half way down the room where I could see all of my audience and they could see me. And I made sure I was positioned against the wall so they would be looking at me and not admiring Melbourne's stunning skyline. As my audience arrived I was able to greet them with the confidence of someone who was in control of the situation.

Control the environment

Another time I was about to give a talk to a social group at the Essendon Football Club where the lectern was in front of a massive glass wall looking over the football field. Not only was this very hard on the eyes, I anticipated that everyone would be more interested in what was happening on the field than behind the lectern! So I said to the organiser, "Do you mind if I move the lectern to the other side of the room, as it would be less of a strain on the eyes for the audience and without distractions they will better be able to see me and hear what I have to say."

She readily agreed to the logic of this suggestion and the whole thing took a couple of minutes. At the end of my talk a lady came up to me and thanked me for being so considerate with my speaking from the other side! She explained that the stark light behind a sil-houetted speaker had been a strain on their eyes for years.

So, don't be afraid to suggest some slight changes if you see that the current set-up is not going to work well.

Tip: If possible, slightly curve the lines of chairs towards the speaker. This will ensure the people on the ends can see clearly.

Handling technology effectively

Not all presentations require you to use technology, but when you do use complicated equipment, it is important you use it effectively. I was once observing a young businessman just before he was about to give a presentation. I remember him picking up a remote control with a lot of buttons on it and saying, "I wonder how this thing works … ?" I also remember him spending the first five minutes of his presentation trying to figure it out!

Tip: Prepare a checklist of your technical equipment and all the bits and pieces you'll be needing on the day. By ticking things off as you go you won't be frantically searching for that plug or special item when you need it.

Thoroughly familiarise yourself with your technology before your presentation. There's nothing worse than a speaker struggling with a laptop or rummaging through a heap of plugs and cords saying, "It must be in here somewhere!" Get in beforehand for a technical run-through and ensure everything works and is precisely where you want it. It is your responsibility to check that everything is in order and ready to go. You'll then have the peace of mind to concentrate your energies on your message and your listeners.

> **Tip:** Make contingency plans. If a piece of equipment decides not to work, don't fiddle with it for five minutes trying to get it to function. Once it's evident you have a problem, maintain listener interest by smoothly shifting to your 'plan B' version of your presentation. And if this fails, revert to your verbal version using stories and case studies to get your message across. Always have a 'plan B' – and even 'C' – up your sleeve.

Using visual aids

Images and charts can offer a refreshing change of pace and are very effective to explain abstract data like statistics or reorganisation procedures. They should, however, reinforce the presentation, not replace it. Reduce each visual display to one idea to keep the minds of your listeners focused on one issue at a time, and make sure your material is brief, in large print and uncluttered. Studies have shown that lower case print is easier to read and understand than upper case.

Always check that your displays can be seen clearly from the back row. I once heard a speaker say, "You probably won't be able to read this so I'll read it for you." Why not prepare it properly in the first place and spare your listeners this boring interlude!

> **Tip:** Introduce at least one main idea with a humorous image. It takes the pressure off you, loosens up your audience, and puts them in the right frame of mind.

Once an image has served its purpose, turn it off! A display relating to a point already covered or a bright empty screen can be very distracting to your listeners. Visual aids should enhance your message, not hinder it.

Whatever technical aids you use to complement your talk, use them sparingly. Don't let them overshadow the person your listeners have come to hear. Sure, a multimedia event could be impressive, but it lacks the warmth of someone communicating on a personal level with stories. Only a real human being can inspire and create rapport with people. Only a real human being can connect with the heart, touch the soul, and paint vivid pictures in the mind. Remember that you are the main act, your technology is your supporting cast. Keep all this in mind when you are preparing your Powerpoint presentations.

Using microphones effectively

How many times have you seen a speaker walk up to the microphone, blow into it and say, "Is this thing working? ... Can you all hear me?" And then proceed to run a series of tests to see if everyone can hear at the back. This technical interlude stems mainly from fear of the microphone and does little to create instant rapport with your listeners. Here's how to avoid it.

Whenever possible, get in early to familiarise yourself with the microphone you'll be using. All microphones are different. It may be on a stand, hand-held, or a lapel version. Take it upon yourself to seek assistance from management or a sound technician if needed. It is critical that you do this. They'll appreciate your interest in doing the best you possibly can. Howling feedback and sound problems can be easily avoided if you get in early and sort it all out. These people are usually more than willing to look after all this for you. Now when you step forward the first thing your listeners will hear are the arresting words of your opening and where you'll be taking them.

"But microphones make me sound funny," people often tell me. The truth is a microphone picks up rich tones and qualities of your voice that aren't normally heard and make you sound 'cool' and professional! I've found that what people really are afraid of is their inner fears and vulnerabilities being amplified for all to hear, not some misguided notion of their weird voice tones! In other words, they're worried about all the unwanted baggage and faulty thinking we dealt with in the early part of this book being magnified for all to see. Here's another truth: the microphone enables you to have a relaxed conversation with a large room full of people, so it's your friend, not your enemy!

Always test the sound system

The day before I was to be Master of Ceremonies of a wedding reception I sought out the manager so I could familiarise myself with the microphone. "Oh, it's all set up and ready to go," he said flippantly, then returned his attention to more important things like directing his staff in setting the tables. He was a busy man.

As my role in the evening was also pivotal, I persisted. "If you don't mind I'd like to get a feel for the microphone to put myself at ease." He handed me a radio microphone and continued with his table setting. When I spoke into it, it sounded great, but when I walked near the head table it made a deafening 'vrooooom' sound. "Watch out over there," the manager called out. "The steel beam above that table interferes with the radio waves."

Tip: Speak over the microphone not into it. Microphones are meant to pick up your voice, not your breathing!

Thanks for telling me, I thought. *Just as well I checked things out!* I now felt at ease with this microphone because I'd gone out of my way to familiarise myself with it. The evening went without a hitch. I made sure that those who used the microphone stayed away from that steel beam. And remember; try not to take anyone else's word that the equipment is correctly set up. When possible give it a little test yourself.

A lot of people find that when they are speaking to a group of 30 or more without a microphone they have to raise their voice to be heard, but when they find themselves before a similar number of people with a microphone they forget to go back to their normal voice level and instead yell at their audience through the microphone.

My wife and I were once guests at a sumptuous wedding reception and for three hours the Master of Ceremonies screamed into the microphone to the point of distorting his voice because he wanted the 500 in attendance to hear him. We couldn't hear ourselves think let alone engage in friendly conversation with those around us. It was a terrible experience. I'm not prone to headaches but I had one that night.

That evening was a disaster because the Master of Ceremonies didn't know that the whole point of using a microphone is to have your audience hear you at a comfortable, conversational level.

Rehearsing your talk in 'virtual reality'

Never would I speak in front of an audience or conduct a workshop without running through my entire talk 'live' a few times before the event. I actually trick my mind into believing I've been with this audience before so that when I step onto the platform the situation is not foreign to me. But what and how does one rehearse?

As someone who has spent many years speaking in front of audiences for a living, here's what I do. I wait until I'm completely alone with no distractions. Then when I'm relaxed in my favourite chair, I imagine myself at the venue where I will be speaking. I see all those friendly people enjoying themselves over dinner and can sense an atmosphere of expectation and excitement.

With this image in mind, I read through my first draft a few times, not to memorise it, but to feel at home with the content, my audience, my all-important bridging thoughts and some key terms and phrases. This phase usually takes two or three sittings of 20 minutes or so. When I am comfortable with this, I reduce my talk down to a few key mental joggers, written or visual and arranged in order. From this point on I rehearse using these key triggers, although I keep my written draft handy to refer to and make ongoing adjustments if necessary. Remember that your talk is not static. It is a dynamic, living thing.

Now I'm ready to rehearse 'live'.

Still visualising myself at the venue, I'm a little nervous and keyed-up but accept this as perfectly normal. As I hear myself being introduced I feel that familiar rush of adrenalin surge through my body. I hear the welcoming applause and confidently step forward as the proud person I am, thank the person who introduced me, and begin to speak. My set opening instantly has them thinking about things I want them to think about, takes the pressure off me and settles me down. The only parts of my talk that are memorised are the opening and closing remarks and the bridging phrases that link my ideas together. In the body of my talk I'm not concerned with the exact words I use, I just mull over my key ideas and let the words flow as they would in normal conversation. I sense the ever-changing mood as I introduce each new idea and involve my listeners in each new story. I see the expression on their faces and feel the warm rapport. Occasionally I toss out a 'feeler' question to keep a little heat on them and check where they are. And each time I rehearse, the words are ever-so-slightly different, giving a spontaneous freshness to my talk. I even anticipate the little asides and the odd ad lib!

I conclude with a carefully chosen story, quote or saying that encapsulates the essence of my message and leaves my listeners with something of substance to think about. As I make my way back to my seat the comments and generous applause tell me that I've appealed to the hearts and minds of my listeners.

The secret is to rehearse your talk for 10 or so minutes each day for at least a week before the event. Rarely do I rehearse the whole talk without a break. I stop and reflect between ideas and add the occasional key word or phrase to my list of mental joggers and first draft as I go. At other times I find myself on my feet talking out loud or interacting with a room full of imaginary, yet 'real' people.

There is one thing that I never do, and that is rehearse in front of a mirror or camera. I find it very off-putting and unnatural. You also run the risk of reinforcing long-held negative beliefs about how bad you look and how awful you sound. "I knew it!" I've heard people lament when they see themselves played back on screen during traditional public speaking training sessions. "I look and sound horrible!" The presence of a camera as a training tool for public speakers can do great damage by further locking in place ingrained self-doubt and anxieties.

Having your talk filmed on the night – from a distance – is fine because this is non-intrusive, but being forced to 'be natural' in front of a camera during a public-speaking training session is quite another matter. We are natural, spontaneous speakers, not actors who are trained to perform to a camera. When rehearsing, my advice is to steer clear of cameras and mirrors as they distract you from being you.

There's one more important thing. On the day of my talk I make sure that my opening words are pretty well off-pat, for what was rehearsed yesterday needs to be refreshed. My list of key mental joggers will keep me on track throughout my talk, but what I say first always needs one last going over on the way to the venue. After all, your set opening is a sure-fire strategy to arrest your listeners' attention and take the pressure off you, so you want to get this right! Now you'll be standing before attentive friends, all primed and eager to hear what you have to say.

Tip: I was once part of a small dinner group hosting an international guest who was to speak at our conference the following day. As we chatted across the table I was very impressed with his knowledge of Australia and the interesting stories he shared. When he spoke the next day I was surprised to hear most of what he'd rehearsed with us over dinner! You can rehearse your stories in everyday conversation with family and friends to gauge their reactions.

Timing your talk

With some speeches you'd swear the speaker has used a calendar to time their talk instead of a clock! To go beyond your allotted time is just plain bad manners. Everyone in your audience has their own commitments and they really appreciate it when you finish on time, so be considerate. Say what you have to say then sit down. If you must extend your talk because specific information is critical to that audience, always ask their permission to do so. But as a rule, if you have five minutes, you have five minutes and not a moment more.

You can either time each segment separately then add them up, or do the whole thing in one hit. Either way, your purpose is to prune your talk to fit the allotted time. And that's the hard part! No matter how precious your information may be to you, if you're running over time you must cut some of it out or condense bits together. Remember, nobody knows how you planned your talk, so they won't know if they have missed out on something. One thing is for sure – they won't appreciate you upsetting their personal timetable. So time yourself to finish on a good note and step down the moment your time is up.

> **Tip:** Avoid having your audience think they have missed out on a valuable piece of information by not saying things like: "If I had more time I would have included ... " or "Unfortunately time's against us so I can't tell you about ... "

Be prepared to give the shortened version of your talk

If, for whatever reason, the program is running over time, spare a thought for your audience and give them a shortened version of your talk. I was once the last of a series of speakers when, because of bad planning and a thoughtless speaker, things were running a long way behind time! I had 45 minutes to wrap up the convention and inspire them to go on to bigger and better things while all my listeners wanted to do was get out of there. My opening words addressed this restlessness: "Ladies and gentlemen, as we are well over time I'm going to say what I have to say in 10 minutes." The applause reflected their frustration – and appreciation! They then heard a briefer version of my talk with an inspirational story that tied it all together. The conference finished on a positive note because I had prepared a shortened version of what I had to say for just such an emergency.

> **Tip:** Keep a small clock on the lectern or table beside you so you can see where you are at a glance. Using your phone is not a good idea, as it may interrupt you unexpectedly, or the screen could go to sleep and then you can't see the clock.

Chapter 9 Key points

- You are responsible for the success of your talk. Get in beforehand to befriend staff in case some 'fine tuning' of room layout is needed.

- Have a 'plan B', even a 'plan C' up your sleeve in case your equipment fails.

- Avoid visual distractions. Turn equipment off when it has served its purpose.

- Where possible get help with a sound test beforehand to familiarise yourself with the microphone and eliminate potential sound problems.

- Each time you rehearse, your words should be ever-so-slightly different to ensure that your talk is a dynamic, living thing.

Monitoring your progress Exercise 9

Agree/Disagree

Consider each of the following statements carefully. Do you agree? Partially agree? Or totally disagree with them? Compare your choice with the Answer Key, page 201 to ensure you leave nothing to chance.

(a) Room layout has little to do with speaking effectiveness.

☐ Agree ☐ Disagree ☐ Partially agree

(b) People are impressed with all the 'bells and whistles' of modern technology. The more multi-media you can make your presentation the more effective you'll be in getting your message across.

☐ Agree ☐ Disagree ☐ Partially agree

(c) Microphones are a speaker's worst enemy. Not only do they make you sound 'funny', they continually play up and interfere with audience rapport.

☐ Agree ☐ Disagree ☐ Partially agree

(d) Every raising of an eyebrow, every intonation, every gesture in your talk must be rehearsed to perfection in front of a mirror for hours. These are the main reasons why people will give up their precious time to come and listen to you.

☐ Agree ☐ Disagree ☐ Partially agree

(e) Keeping to the allotted time for your talk is crucial. People really appreciate it when you say what you have to say in the allotted time then sit down. You'll win few friends if you go over time and upset their commitments.

☐ Agree ☐ Disagree ☐ Partially agree

Check your answers and learn!

CHAPTER 10

Tying it all together

Johan Devres tells a story that neatly sums up the essence of this journey of renewal. As a young lad in his native Holland he was a passionate ice skater. One crisp, winter evening as he was speed skating home along a frozen waterway he got the shock of his life. He remembers thinking of the nice warm fire and hearty meal that awaited him as he swept round a bend. Without warning something crashed into his chest as he plowed through a workman's barrier. Everything went black and before he knew it he was sinking to the bottom of the icy canal. *I've got to get out of this*, he thought. *I don't want to die!* By now his skates were sticking in the mud and his air was almost gone. With a super-human effort he forced his way to the surface, only to hit his head on the roof of his icy tomb. Panic-stricken, he began clawing his way along the slippery bank beneath the ice trying to find the hole he had fallen through. But nothing! Just more ice! Gasping for breath from the small space of air between the ice and the water surface, and strength almost gone, he began to choke. Just as he was about to succumb to the icy fingers that beckoned him down to a watery grave his head bobbed through the hole and an unknown hand pulled him to safety.

Years later, as a young man in his twenties living in Australia, Johan found himself at the seaside with his mates. Although wearing a bathing costume, it was sheer pretence for he had never been in the water since that day. "Come on Johan!" one of his friends called out, "Let's swim back to camp instead of walking across the bridge." Everyone thought this a great idea and headed for the water. Johan froze.

The jig was up. He was about to be found out! The terrible fear he'd fended off all these years was upon him and dragging him down into that icy grave again. He found it hard to breathe and was trembling all over. Johan had two choices: either walk back across that bridge and live with his fears for the rest of his life, or face them head on and follow his friends into the water. Weeping openly Johan raced across the beach and plunged in.

He recalls feeling a cold, clammy sweat pouring off him even under water. On he powered, oblivious to what was happening around him, each stroke leaving a little more of his long-held fears behind him. When he reached the opposite shore he leapt out of the water like a swimmer at the Olympics. "I felt like a million dollars," he told me later. Purged of the fear that had hounded him for years he's enjoyed the water ever since.

And Johan's inspirational story of facing his fears is similar to your journey of being prisoner to the public speaking fear that has been holding you back for so long. Now that you've identified the *causes* of your conditioned anxieties and self-imposed limitations you are able to plunge in and courageously swim to freedom just as Johan did. And as your understanding of yourself and your communicating confidence grows, you will gain more and more courage to keep swimming strongly across that stretch of water instead of walking back across the bridge and feeling like a defeated loser. And guess what? The further you distance yourself from those debilitating fears, the more placid the water gets! Soon the whole painful experience will be nothing but a distant memory ...

As a result of this mind-opening approach your thinking has irreversibly changed. You now have an 'enlightened' view of what public speaking that warmly connects with people is all about. Not only have you discovered the natural speaker that already exists in you, you now have the practical know-how, self belief, and tools to do the job!

So where to from here?

One final word: it's important to keep in mind that every once in a while your old uncertainty will come knocking on your door trying to wedge its foot in and drag you back to the fearful place you used to be. Here's the simple solution to keep yesterday's public speaking anxieties at bay so they never get the chance to ruin your life again.

Like someone learning to play a musical instrument you've got to be consistent. It's no good practising a solid four hours every two months with nothing in between. A consistent visit to these pages for ideas and inspirations on a daily basis is the key. Five to ten minutes a day is all you need. Even reading one page a day will do the trick! This will keep these mind-opening ideas in the forefront of your mind so you're ready for the daily communicating challenges that face us all. And in a short space of time you'll realise that there was nothing inherently wrong with your communicating potential at all. All you needed was a bit of help to see things differently.

And the good thing about this life-changing journey of discovery is it never ends.

Appendices

Planning your talk

This section will guide you through the simple steps of creating a dynamic presentation for that all-important occasion. All too often a self-help guide is read once then left to gather dust on the shelf, but rather than just reading about it, you can use this section to actually help you plan your talk. With these pages you will be able to put what you have learnt to practical use.

You may want to duplicate these pages to give you some spares as you practise. And remember, it's perfectly normal to feel a little apprehensive as you begin. This is the system I use as a professional speaker to plan my presentations and this is the system I used to write this book. By carefully and thoughtfully completing these steps, you will end up with the outline of an interesting talk you feel comfortable with.

The fundamentals

Describe the topic:

_____

_____

_____

_____

_____

_____

_____

_____

_____

Describe the occasion and the setting:

_____
_____
_____
_____
_____
_____
_____
_____
_____

Describe the people you will be speaking to:

_____
_____
_____
_____
_____
_____
_____
_____
_____

Brainstorming

On a separate piece of paper, brainstorm your topic using the questions below as a guide. At this stage don't be judgmental. Give your mind free rein by letting your thoughts flow freely around the central idea of meeting your listeners' needs. Keep in mind the setting and the location.

- If you were in your listeners' shoes, what would you want to know? How would you want to feel?

- What do you perceive to be the areas of common-interest for these specific people?

- What are their hopes, dreams, wants and desires?

- What are some needs they are not aware of?

This will give you inspiration to formulate your 'focus sentence' for this audience – the overall message for your talk. In a single statement, answer the question, "What is the precise purpose of this talk?", or, "What is the main message I want to get across?" (I find this sentence comes much easier if I say it out loud before I attempt to write it down.)

My focus sentence for this talk will be:

_____

_____

_____

_____

_____

My approach will be (keep in mind who your listeners are and the nature of the occasion):

_____

_____

_____

_____

_____

_____

_____

_____

_____

_____

The title of my talk is:
(List several possibilities, and then choose one as a working title. Make it catchy and appealing to your listeners' interests. Draw inspiration from online content and advertising material.)

_____

_____

_____

_____

_____

_____

_____

_____

_____

_____

Outlining your talk

On a separate piece of paper, write your 'focus sentence' at the top of the page to keep your mind on the central purpose and 'destination'/conclusion of your talk and what you want to accomplish. Then write your title in the middle of the page and 'branch' related ideas off it in a logical clockwise sequence. You might have to change the sequence of these ideas around until you are happy with them. Now you have a preliminary outline of where your talk is going (the purpose) and the interesting points along the way. Draw ideas from this general outline for a fully laid out plan of your talk.

Talk plan

Using your general outline as a guide, complete the following template for a fully laid out plan of your talk. Start by again writing down your 'focus sentence' to keep your destination firmly in mind.

Attention grabbing opener (example): "How many people here have ever had trouble putting an interesting talk together? Well look no further … Tonight you're going to learn a magic Four-Step Formula to make planning a presentation a breeze … "

1. Determine your destination:

    •   Write down your focus sentence.

    •   Plan your opening comments around your focus sentence.

    •   Explain how your topic is relevant to your listeners.

2. Set up mental signposts:

    •   Keep your central purpose in mind.

    •   Avoid information overload.

    •   Set up your mental signposts, four or five must-knows.

3. Provide vivid examples to support what you are saying:

    •   Quote experts.

    •   Provide a real-life example/demonstration/story.

    •   Use symbols/objects to jog your memory and support what you are saying.

4. Motivate your listeners to think and act:

    •   Relate your conclusion to your focus sentence.

    •   End your presentation with impact; for example, use humour, drama or a quote from an expert.

    •   Provide a real-life example/story.

    •   Throw down a challenge.

And finally, familiarise yourself with the situation and your audience before the event by rehearsing your talk (see chapter 9, 'Leave Nothing to Chance').

Presentation checklist

A presentation checklist will help you prepare for this particular audience in this particular setting before you begin planning. Points to consider are:

- [ ] Purpose of gathering (staff meeting, award night, etc.)
- [ ] Start time and length of your talk
- [ ] Who will introduce you
- [ ] Prepare your introduction
- [ ] Size of audience (are partners included?)
- [ ] Audience details – average age, gender ratio
- [ ] General description of audience (who are they?)
- [ ] Description of room and seating format
- [ ] Background of the organisation
- [ ] VIPs in attendance
- [ ] Sensitive issues to be avoided
- [ ] What did they like or dislike about past speakers
- [ ] What positive comments would you expect to overhear at the end of your talk

Meeting action statement

Chairperson:
Present:
Objective of meeting:

Action	Who	Due date	☑
			☐
			☐
			☐
			☐
			☐
			☐
			☐
			☐
			☐
			☐

Answer key

Correct answers to exercise 2

1. False: Speakers who try to 'wing it' invariably end up losing their way and their listeners' attention. A carefully thought out talk gives you the inner confidence of knowing where you want to go and how you're going to take your listeners there.

2. False: Your opening remarks and the words that immediately follow are just as important as your concluding thoughts. They set the appropriate atmosphere and put people in the right frame of mind for something special – as well as take the pressure off you! Your final words will pack a lot more impact when you've whet your listeners' appetite for what's to follow at the start of your talk.

3. True: Transitional words and phrases make it easy for people to move from one thought to the next without losing their way. Without these smooth links from one main idea to the next, your talk would come across as a series of unconnected ideas where your audience struggles to make sense of it all. A transitional phrase like: "Now that we know how it functions, let's look at how to install it", smoothly transfers their thinking to your next idea as you carry your theme forward.

4. False: Vivid illustrative examples humanise sterile information and bring it to life! Rather than detract from the real message, they enhance it!

Correct answers to exercise 4

Your answers will be worded differently than the following sample answers. However, your main ideas should be about the same.

1. Your main focus will be on the message you want to get across. An understanding of your audience, even if only superficial, will determine the approach you take.

2. Arrange a meeting with the organiser to learn about your audience, their interests, and what they expect from you. You could achieve the same thing by way of a presentation checklist (see sample on page 194). You could phone two or three members of your audience to sound out their views on the expected take-home value of your talk. Or you could do a search online to learn more about the organisation.

3. The three main characteristics that naturally occur in everyday conversation are mental pictures, feelings, and hearing (paraphrasing what was said or thought). You'll include these three traits in every talk you'll ever give by telling stories and sharing case studies because these characteristics are the natural triggers that set off the sensory 'hot buttons' in your audience and cause them to sit up and listen!

4. From now on you'll no longer compare yourself to the communicating talents of this person or be overwhelmed by them. You'll coolly evaluate just what it is they're doing and learn from them. You'll be inspired to compare yourself to your own potential and build on your own talents.

5. His ultimate impression of you is: "Here is someone with initiative who gets along with people and communicates with confidence! Here is someone who could inspire and lead our team from out front … the very type of person we're after!"

Correct answers to exercise 5

Several possible answers are given here. Since your answers may not be worded the same as the following model answers, use your own judgment in marking yourself right or wrong.

1. The majority of our fears reside in our heads and nowhere else! We alone have the power to cast them out forever and start walking a new path of communicating confidence!

2. Technical body language comes across as staged and mechanical. Believable body language has that intuitive quality we identify in everyday conversation.

3. Talking to the right ideas will ensure your talk is a dynamic living thing in harmony with the rapport of the audience. You'll be at one with your listeners instead of sweating on that 'right' word to appear.

4. If you lose your train of thought, as all humans are apt to do, don't let on. Simply glance at your next key idea and bridge into it as if this break is the most natural thing in the world. Coolly stroll over to your glass of water, take a sip, and steal a glance at your notes right beside it. Then bridge into your next idea. And remember that people don't see these pauses as problems with the speaker. They think they're deliberate to give the audience time to reflect on what's been said.

5. Television newsreaders read everything they say from a teleprompter. They are polished clean to give the impression of a flawless speaker. In reality, they have little in common with the natural dynamics of speaking before a live audience.

6. Forget the self-effacing apologies at the beginning of a talk. They turn people off and give the impression that the speaker lacks confidence and self-worth. Always start on a positive note and get straight into your talk.

7. When you look people in the eye everyone feels comfortable. Your eyes are the windows to your soul. They radiate sincerity, self-worth, trust, and connect you with the emotions of your listeners.

Correct answers to exercise 6

1. No: Your central theme and the principles your examples embody must mean something to this particular audience. Now your passion and enthusiasm will ignite their interest.

2. No: The objective of an effective communicator is to connect with people. Speakers who trade an occasional 'aside' with their audience are connecting with them on a human level.

3. Yes: Metaphors don't single anybody out and enable people to save face. People see the folly of their ways in the stories of others.

4. Yes: Audiences sit up and listen when they perceive there's something in it for them.

Correct answers to exercise 7

Your answers are right if they reflect similar ideas to the following sample answers.

1. (a): You could say something like: "And how could we survive without you folk in the warehouse to back us up in getting our products safely to the client … On the rare occasion where we've had a slip up we've worked together as a professional team to fix the problem." You'd then relate from memory a brief example that illustrates this.

(b): You could replay a harmless incident you witnessed at the after-conference dinner where everyone let their hair down. Or something funny that happened at the product launch, award night, or the Christmas get-together. Naturally you'll be tactful in your choice of example and ensure it in no way offends.

(c): Mindful that these people are gathered to wish you well for the future, you'll express your heartfelt thanks for the friendship and thoughtfulness you've experienced while working with them. You'll evidence these thoughts with examples they can relate to.

2. (a): His purpose is to highlight his friend's musical genius and readiness to always share with others.

(b): The 'Past, Present, Future' formula takes his fellow mourners on a brief journey from the time he met his friend to the morning he learnt of his untimely death on social media. He purposefully included a humorous anecdote to relieve tension and remind people of the lighter side of life. He concluded by pointing to the future with a story of inspiration and hope. And he mentally rehearsed his talk, determined not to apologise for his natural feelings of sadness.

3. (a): It's a question of knowing who your audience are. When speaking to his conservative colleagues in the halls of academia the professor's tone would reflect this learned setting. That's not to say he can't humanise what he's saying. But with an after-dinner talk to a general audience the atmosphere is of a lighter nature. Here, people don't want to be educated, they want to be entertained!

(b): Three reasons why you'd enjoy this talk could be: The intriguing title promises a light-hearted approach; the speaker plans to have a bit of fun by drawing on the collective wit of the audience; and everyone enjoys an amusing story.

Correct answers to exercise 8

(a): Prepare something; (b): Past, Present, Future; (c): Personally; (d): Controversial, positive; (e): Capture, curiosity; (f): Audience; (g): Honest; (h): Cool, argument; (i) Conclusion.

Correct answers to exercise 9

Consider your answers correct if they mean something similar to the answer key.

(a) Partially agree: Some stirring speeches are delivered in adverse conditions, but why make things difficult for yourself? Being at the venue early to make sure the room is exactly how you want it will free you to concentrate on your message and your listeners.

(b) Disagree: Only human beings can connect with the heart as well as the mind. Only human beings can stir our emotions with the spoken word. Use technology to complement your talk, not supplement it.

(c) Disagree: Microphones are a speaker's best friend. They enhance the quality of your voice, make you sound professional, and enable you to 'converse' with a large audience. The secret is to get in early and sort out all the bugs before you get up to speak.

(d) Disagree: People are not motivated in the least by the cold mechanics and technicalities of speaking. They give up their precious time to be informed, entertained, inspired or persuaded.

(e) Agree: If your time has elapsed, your audience is not interested in you giving them 'a few extra ideas'. They expect you to finish on time.

About Laurie Smale

"Being the Confident Speaker You Want to Be!"

Laurie Smale's credentials in setting you firmly on your new path of communicating confidence are well-earned for he's also suffered the fear, panic, sweaty palms, knocking knees and debilitating effects of more than one humiliating public speaking or conversational disaster! But no more. As a person who now confidently communicates with people and coaches speakers for a living – and has done so for decades – he's packaged a lifetime of practical wisdom into seven mind-opening books and audio programs, including his new second edition of his classic bestseller *How to Take The Panic out of Public Speaking*, and his latest self-help book *Finding Me Finding You*, all of which embody everything you've ever wanted to know about communicating effectiveness. His tried-and-proven ideas and inspirations will show you how easy it can be to believe in yourself and feel calm and confident as an interesting all-round communicator – whatever the situation – for he's been through all the painful trial and error for you.

Check them out, and his comprehensive package deal, at
www.panicfreepublicspeaking.com.au.

www.ingramcontent.com/pod-product-compliance
Lightning Source LLC
Chambersburg PA
CBHW071210210326
41597CB00016B/1754